THE VIKINGS

VOYAGERS OF DISCOVERY AND PLUNDER

THE VIKINGS

VOYAGERS OF DISCOVERY AND PLUNDER

Foreword by Magnus Magnusson

R Chartrand · K Durham · M Harrison · I Heath

First published in Great Britain in 2006 by Osprey Publishing Ltd.
This paperback edition first published in 2008 by Osprey Publishing Ltd,
Midland House, West Way, Botley, Oxford OX2 0PH, United Kingdom.
443 Park Avenue South, New York, NY 10016, USA.
Email: info@ospreypublishing.com

Previously published as Ian Heath, Elite 3: *The Vikings*; Mark Harrison, Warrior 3: *Viking Hersir 793–1066 AD*; and Keith Durham, New Vanguard 47: *Viking Longship*

A CIP catalogue record for this book is available from the British Library

ISBN: 978-1-84603-340-7

Page layout by Ken Vail Graphic Design, Cambridge, UK
Index by Alison Worthington
Maps by The Map Studio
Originated by United Graphics Pte Ltd, Singapore
Printed in China through Worldprint Ltd

08 09 10 11 12   10 9 8 7 6 5 4 3 2 1

For a catalogue of all books published by Osprey please contact:

NORTH AMERICA
Osprey Direct c/o Random House Distribution Center
400 Hahn Road, Westminster, MD 21157, USA
E-mail: info@ospreydirect.com

ALL OTHER REGIONS
Osprey Direct UK, P.O. Box 140, Wellingborough, Northants, NN8 2FA, UK
E-mail: info@ospreydirect.co.uk

www.ospreypublishing.com

Front cover: Replica of a Viking ship. (© Topham Pictureport/TopFoto)
Back cover: Viking helmet. (© Museum of Cultural History, University of Oslo, Norway, photographer Ove Holst)
Title page: A selection of Lewis chessmen (© C M Dixon/The Ancient Art & Architecture Collection Ltd)
Celtic design pp. 10, 82 and 142: (© Courtney Davis, www.celtic-art.com)
Longship pp. 5, 6 and 9: (© Harald Faith-Ell/Antivarisk–Topografiska Arkivet, National Heritage Board, Stockholm)k

Osprey Publishing is supporting the Woodland Trust, the leading UK woodland conservation charity, by funding the dedication of trees.

CONTENTS

FOREWORD BY MAGNUS MAGNUSSON   6

CHRONOLOGY   9

A HISTORY OF THE VIKINGS   10

THE VIKING HERSIR   82

THE VIKING LONGSHIP   142

GLOSSARY   196

BIBLIOGRAPHY   198

APPENDIX   200

INDEX   202

FOREWORD
By Magnus Magnusson

I had better come clean at once: I am a professional Viking apologist. I have long laboured in the groves of Viking revisionism. In short, as far as I am concerned, Vikings Rule.

The so-called 'Viking Age' began around AD 800 and lasted for nearly three centuries. In the pages of history, it is presented as a clearly defined period of high drama, with a theatrical curtain-raiser, a long middle act of mounting power and ferocity all over Europe, and a spectacular finale on a battlefield in England. The dates are clear cut, too: 793 to 1066. And throughout that time, war correspondents in the shape of literate monks and clerics kept their goose-quill pens sharpened with alarm, their glossy inks dyed bright with indignation. The Vikings were cast in the role of Antichrist: merciless barbarians who plundered and burned their way across the known world, heedless of their own lives or the lives of others, intent only on destruction and pillage. Their sinister emblems were Thor's hammer and Odin's raven, symbolizing the violence and black-hearted evil of their pagan gods.

It was never as one-sided as that – history seldom is. But it made a good story at the time, and it makes a good story still. It was by no means the whole story, however. Today there is emerging a much fuller and rounder version (mainly through modern archaeology, but with the help of other scientific and literary disciplines as well) – a version that presents the Vikings in a less lurid and more objective light. It is a matter of emphasis: less emphasis on the raiding, more on the trading; less on the pillage, more on the poetry and the artistry; less on the terror, more on the technology of these dynamic people from the northlands and on the positive impact they had on the countries they affected.

This book – *The Vikings: Voyagers of Discovery and Plunder* – is presented in three sumptuously illustrated parts. The profuse photographs are given informative captions, and the historical reconstructions are sensible and do not strive for melodramatic effect. The 'apparatus' is equally effective: a chronology, a glossary of technical terms, a select bibliography and an appendix naming the major relevant museums in Britain and Scandinavia.

From it, a clear picture emerges of the changing face of the Viking world, and the changing face of the Vikings. 'Who were the Vikings?' asks the first section, 'A History of the Vikings'. And not only who were they, but what were they? In short, they were piratical opportunists of Norse stock, from the three major Scandinavian countries, which became Norse kingdoms – Denmark, Norway and Sweden. In the same way as the Elizabethan Age in England could be called the 'Privateering Age', so the Viking Age in the northlands could be labelled the 'Piracy Age'.

Socially, these Norsemen were primarily independent farmers or fishermen; merchants or craftsmen; blacksmiths or carpenters. They owed allegiance to local aristocratic chieftains, or *jarls* (earls), who in turn owed loyalty to the king. Right at the bottom of the social pyramid were the thralls (slaves), who were owned body and soul by their masters and lived lives of back-breaking servitude. The slave-trade was highly lucrative, and slave markets flourished as far afield as Dublin and Constantinople.

Women in the Viking Age played an unusually positive role in society by medieval standards. They were feisty frontierswomen in spirit and action, and in almost every respect held equal status with their menfolk. They had complete authority over all household matters, and had 'liberated' legal rights far in advance of the times, such as the right to divorce and a claim to half the marital property. They made their presence felt – often, quite literally, with a vengeance.

Part two, 'The Viking Hersir', opens with the heading, 'A culture of violence'. Violence was undoubtedly the stock-in-trade of the Norsemen. In time, it was channelled into controlled state violence, as the Scandinavian countries embraced Christianity one by one and embarked on imperialist military adventures. Denmark, under Svein Forkbeard and his son Cnut (Knútr), conquered much of England and forced the partition of England with the creation of the 'Danelaw'. Sweden made inroads into the depths of Russia, founding city-states like Novgord and Kiev, pioneering new trade routes along formidable rivers like the Volga and the Dnieper, and opening the route to Asia to exploit the exotic markets of Persia and China.

The third section, 'The Viking Longship', traces the story of Viking seafaring. The Norsemen were extraordinary mariners. They criss-crossed half the world in their open boats and vastly extended its known boundaries; they voyaged farther north and west than any Europeans had ever been before, founding new and lasting colonies in the Faroe Islands and Iceland, and discovering, exploring and making settlements in Greenland and even North America.

Their lightweight ships gave them enormous tactical mobility. Their naval engagements were simply extensions of land battles: their fleets were roped together, gunwale to gunwale, to form floating platforms. From then on, the fighting was a grim process of attrition until the opposing ship had been cleared and all its crew killed.

But it was not the lean and predatory longship, lordly and menacing, that played the starring role in the last fling of Viking expansion westwards; it was the sturdy, swan-breasted cargo ship, the *knarr*, the maid of all work of the high seas. It was the *knarr* that carried the explorers and would-be settlers of North America in search of Vinland the Good, 'Wineland', the fabled Promised Land somewhere on the eastern shore of Canada and the United States. The *knarr* was the last heroine of the astonishing Viking seafaring adventure.

What a tapestry this book presents! What a splendid pageant of history and story!

CHRONOLOGY

c. 350 BC	Hjortspring boat sunk in a bog in southern Denmark as a votive offering.
c. AD 350–400	Nydam ship sunk in south Jutland as a sacrificial offering.
c. 700	Kvalsund ship built.
789	Killing of King Beorhtric's reeve by Vikings.
792	Offa prepares defences of Kent against 'pagan seamen'.
793	Raid on Lindisfarne.
795	Raid on Iona.
799	Viking raiders off the mouth of the Loire.
c. 800	Oseberg ship built.
810	Danish assault on Frisia.
830–850	Raids on the French coast and southern England.
c. 834	Oseberg ship interred in Vestfold, Norway.
835	Vikings land in West Country, defeated by Egbert, king of West Saxons.
c. 850	Birth of Harald Harfagri.
851	First time a Viking army winters in England – at Thanet.
865	First English Danegeld paid by inhabitants of Kent.
867	Ragnar's sons attack and take York.
c. 870	Harald Harfagri sole king of Norway. Vikings reach and settle Iceland.
c. 872	Battle of Hafrsfjord.
877	Fall of Mercia to Vikings.
879	Fall of East Anglia.
886	Treaty between Guthrum and Alfred. Siege of Paris.
c. 890	Gokstad ship built.
895–905	Egil Skallagrimson born.
930–937	Resurgence of Wessex dynasty to unitary monarchy.
937	Battle of Brunanburh.
940–954	Intermittent independence for the Viking kingdom of York.
978	Accession of Ethelred II.
980	Renewed Viking raids on England.
c. 985	Death of Egil Skallagrimson.
c. 986	Erik the Red founds Eastern and Western colonies in Greenland.
991	Battle of Maldon.
991–1015	Extortion of massive Danegelds. Thorkell the Tall (Jomsviking) active in England. Swein asserts Danish mastery of England.
c. 1000	Viking settlement at L'Anse aux Meadows, Newfoundland.
1014	Battle of Clontarf.
1016–35	Reign of Cnut. The 'Viking Empire' of the North Sea.
c. 1025	Roskilde 6 built.
c. 1030–50	Skuldelev 1 built in western Norway.
c. 1040	Skuldelev 3 built.
1043–66	Reign of Edward the Confessor. The battle of Stamford Bridge.
1085	Collapse of Swein Estridson's expedition to eastern England. The end of the Scandinavian threat.

A History of the Vikings

WHO WERE THE VIKINGS?

789: In this year King Beorhtric took to wife Eadburh, daughter of King Offa. And in his days there came for the first time three ships of Northmen, from Hörthaland: and the reeve rode thither and tried to compel them to go to the royal manor — for he did not know what they were — and they slew him. These were the first ships of the Danes to come to England.

Thus the *Anglo-Saxon Chronicle* reports the first raid, and the first victim, of the Vikings. Four years later, in AD 793, there followed the much more famous raid on the island monastery at Lindisfarne: 'The harrying of the heathen miserably destroyed God's church in Lindisfarne by rapine and slaughter.' 'Never before has such terror appeared in Britain as we have now suffered from a pagan race', wrote the contemporary scholar Alcuin, 'nor was it thought possible that such an inroad from the sea could be made. Behold the church of St Cuthbert, spattered with the blood of the priests of God, despoiled of all its ornaments; a place more venerable than any other in Britain has fallen prey to pagans.'

This depiction of the Vikings as blood-thirsty pagans had its roots in an earlier conception of the 'barbaric north'. To classical authors of the Mediterranean, the world was balanced perfection. The hot, dry, bright and civilized south found its opposite in the cold, wet, dark and barbaric north. The first inkling the Romans had that the two were not in perfect harmony was when the Cimbri and Teutones moved into southern Gaul in around 100 BC. The Romans understood these tribes to have originated in the Danish peninsula, but the nerve centre of threat to the empire was located further north. The destructive Ostrogoths and Visigoths are described by Jordanes as economic refugees from the overcrowded Baltic island of Gotland.

This Scandinavian dimension to the barbarian menace survived the collapse of the Roman Empire. The Frankish successor state, the main inheritor of Roman traditions, found the far northerners increasingly threatening as time passed. The expedition of Hygelac the Geat to the Rhineland, recorded

The seaborne warriors in this illustration from the 'Life of St Aubin' probably give a good impression of the appearance of the more 'professional' warriors of the later Viking Age. (Bibliothèque nationale de France / NAL 1390)

by Gregory of Tours and in the anonymous *Beowulf*, appears to be an isolated incident. As the Carolingians gained control over central and northern Germany, and thus came into contact with the southern borders of Danish settlement, the Vikings enter into the historical record with what appears to be a sudden and catastrophic impact.

When describing Scandinavia on the eve of the Viking Age it is difficult to avoid spuriously dividing it into three nations: Danish, Norwegian and Swedish. This division is largely a product of medieval history. The major difference between the various Viking homelands was the linguistic one of East and West Norse dialects. This picture is further complicated by an early emergence of centralized monarchy in Denmark. Signs of state formation above the level of clan and tribe can be seen in *The Frankish Royal Annals*. When Godfred of Denmark submitted to Charlemagne it was, in the mind of the chronicler, on behalf of a unified Danish kingdom. The power of the early Danish monarchy is plain to see in the refurbishment of the Danevirke, a massive, pre-Viking line of fortifications separating Jutland from mainland Europe. Only a regime of some wealth and power could have initiated such extensive work.

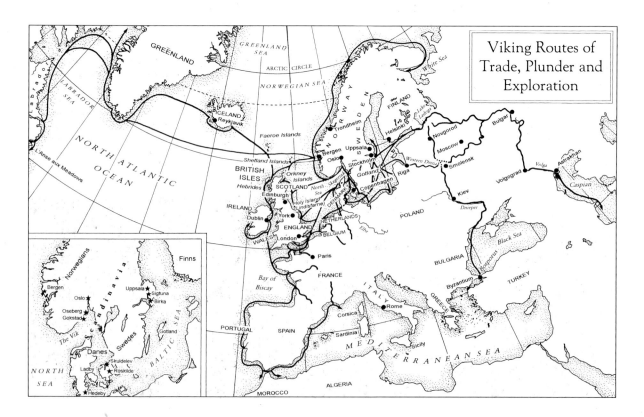

Viking Routes of Trade, Plunder and Exploration

The Frankish Royal Annals further note that Godfred's kingdom included the area of Vestfold. Although the writer placed this overseas province in Britain, it was in fact part of Norway. The Danish foothold in Vestfold can be seen as the beginning of Danish domination of Norway. It also led directly to the early emergence of a Norwegian monarchy under King Harald in the 9th century.

To the Anglo-Saxons, then, the Vikings were 'pagans', 'Danes' or 'Northmen', the term 'Viking' itself being rarely used in sources outside of Scandinavia (even though it has been suggested by some scholars that the word derives from Saxon *wic*, a military encampment). Frankish sources too refer to them as *Nordmanni* ('Northmen' or 'Normans'); while German chroniclers describe them as *Ascomanni* ('Ashmen', an unexplained description which, it has been suggested, may have derived from some of their ships being constructed of ash trees, even though most were of oak). Spanish Moslem sources refer to them as *al-Madjus* ('heathen wizards'); Slavic sources as *Rus* (possibly from the Finnish name for Sweden, *Rotsi*); and Byzantine sources as *Rhos* (from the Greek adjective for red, because of their ruddy complexions) or *Varangoi* (probably from Old Norse *var*, 'pledge', describing a band of men who had sworn loyalty to one another). Only the Irish, who referred to them as *Lochlannach* ('Northerners') or *Gaill* ('strangers' or 'foreigners'), actually attempted to distinguish between Norwegians (*Finn-gaill*, 'white foreigners') and Danes (*Dubh-gaill*, 'black foreigners'), chroniclers of other nations tending to use the terms 'Danes', 'Norwegians', and even 'Swedes', interchangeably. For example, Adam of Bremen, writing *c.* 1075, refers to 'the Danes and the Swedes whom we call Norsemen or Northmen'; and also tells us that 'the Danes and the Swedes and the other peoples beyond Denmark [i.e., the Norwegians] are called Norsemen'. Therefore when the *Anglo-Saxon Chronicle* repeatedly refers to *Dene* or *Dani*, it should not be assumed that the Vikings in question necessarily originated in Denmark.

The lid of the Franks Casket, produced in Northumbria in the early 8th century. Though pre-Viking, it is easy to imagine that scenes like this, of a man defending his house against armed raiders, were commonplace from the late 8th century onwards. (CM Dixon / The Ancient Art & Architecture Collection Ltd)

The actual origin of the word 'Viking' is not known with absolute certainty, though there are a growing number of scholars who favour a derivation from *vik* (an inlet, fjord or bay), which would make a Viking 'a pirate hidden in a fjord or inlet'. Other suggestions derive it from the geographical region of Vik in Norway; or else from *vig* (a battle, which is unlikely on phonological grounds); or from *vikja* (meaning to move or turn aside), making a Viking 'one who makes a detour'. In written Scandinavian sources *viking* actually means piracy or a pirate raid, while a man participating in such a foray was actually called a *vikingr*.

Suggested reasons for the sudden appearance of the Vikings at the end of the 8th century are many and varied. Overpopulation at home is usually cited as one of the prime factors, a population explosion having occurred in Norway and, more particularly, Denmark in the course of the 7th–8th centuries. In addition, the gradual establishment of firm government throughout much of Western Europe, especially on the Continent with the foundation of the Carolingian Empire under Charlemagne, had resulted in a considerable increase in European mercantile trade, which led in turn to increased opportunities for piracy. Undoubtedly connected with this was the stage of evolution that had been reached in the Scandinavian art of shipbuilding in the course of the 8th century. This had resulted not only in the justly famous longships which we invariably associate with the Vikings, but also in the less well-known *knarrs*, or merchant vessels; in these respectively the Vikings were able to raid far afield and, subsequently, to colonize the lands they found. They were the very tools of Viking expansion.

THE VIKINGS AT HOME

Viking society

In spite of their enduring image as ruthless raiders and dauntless explorers, most Vikings were primarily farmers, fishermen, merchants, shipbuilders, craftsmen, blacksmiths or carpenters.

Many of them, however, were able to lead a life that combined elements of both existences. Traditional oral histories, or 'sagas', which were consigned to manuscripts in Iceland at the beginning of the 11th century, relate details of the Viking way of life. In the *Orkneyinga Saga* we are told that a 12th-century Norse chieftain, Svein Asleifsson, who lived on the Isle of Orkney, would spend the winter at home and set out in the spring:

> … and in the spring he had more than enough to occupy him, with a great deal
> of seed to sow which he saw to carefully himself. Then when that job was done,

Scandinavian warrior, 6th–7th centuries. This figure is based on the spearmen depicted on the Torslunda plates from pre-Viking Sweden. The middle-status warrior pictured here died over a hundred years before the attack on Lindisfarne and in that respect is an 'ancestor' of the Vikings. (Gerry Embleton © Osprey Publishing Ltd)

Items of Viking personal jewellery found at Chessell Down, Isle of Wight: beads of glass, amber, crystal and paste. (© Copyright the Trustees of the British Museum)

he would go off plundering in the Hebrides and in Ireland on what he called his 'spring-trip'; then back home just after midsummer, where he stayed till the cornfields had been reaped and the grain was safely in. After that he would go off raiding again, and never came back till the first month of winter was ended. This he called his 'autumn-trip'.

While voyaging abroad on raiding or trading expeditions in the company of like-minded Norsemen, a land-owning freeman such as Svein Asleifsson would doubtless have agreed that he and his fellows had no master, but were 'all equal', a proud assertion that has become a defining aspect of Viking culture. At home, however, men such as Asleifsson were actually part of a highly stratified, pyramidal society.

At the apex of this pyramid stood the king. Below him were the aristocracy, the *jarls*, military leaders and powerful landowners with extensive holdings. Beneath them were the freemen, or *bóndis*. This diverse group, which consisted of farmers, merchants, shipwrights, skilled craftsmen and professional warriors, comprised the largest and perhaps most influential class in Viking Age society, their social status being determined by the extent of their wealth. At the base of the pyramid were the slaves, or thralls, who were often regarded by their owners as little more than animals, and as a rule, were treated in much the same manner.

At the beginning of the Viking Age, authority within Scandinavia rested in the hands of a small number of powerful, well-established families, each controlling large tracts of land. In time, amidst shifting alliances, propitious marriages and often by force of arms, single-ruling dynasties began to emerge in Norway, Denmark and Sweden.

The king

In the Viking Age, royal wealth was accumulated both by conquest and from the king's extensive estates, which were administered by his representatives. These holdings were scattered throughout the realm and in addition to providing revenue, served as convenient bases, providing shelter and sustenance for the king and his entourage as they travelled through the kingdom. Revenue was also obtained by way of taxes, in the form of customs duty and market tolls, which were collected by the king's officials in towns and harbours that came within royal jurisdiction. The king, in his turn, had certain obligations to his subjects, and it was in his own best interest to ensure that as far as was possible in such times, merchants could carry out their business without fear of disruption or attack.

That Scandinavian royalty and their aristocracy lived well is evident from the quality of their grave goods, such as those excavated at Oseberg and Gokstad. Kings in particular would have surrounded themselves with objects and equipment of great beauty, and royal patronage would have extended to skilled craftsmen of all kinds. Carpenters, shipwrights, wood carvers, artist-craftsmen, armourers and silversmiths would all have shared the benefit of royal wealth.

A significant part of the king's income must have been necessary to finance the *hird*, his standing army of professional warriors. Often housed in purpose-built barracks, such as those at Trelleborg and Fyrkat, their presence, although costly, was essential for any number of reasons, not least of which was to hold in check his own powerful and ambitious *jarls*. Command of the *hird* would only have been entrusted to a member of the king's immediate family, or a *jarl* whose allegiance to the crown was beyond question. Within the king's inner circle of retainers, other prominent figures would have included a master of stables, who was responsible for the royal horses, and a master mariner, who would have maintained the king's fleet. No royal entourage would have been complete, however, without the regular attendance of a skald. Highly respected and favoured with extravagant gifts and hospitality, these travelling poets would enshrine the king's exploits in artful, rhythmic verse and praise his generosity. As they travelled the length and breadth of the land, these poems would be recited at farmsteads, feasts and gatherings, thus ensuring news of the king's deeds spread far and wide and that hopefully, word of his fame was passed down from generation to generation.

By the end of the 10th century, thriving trade and the consolidation of royal power in Norway, Denmark and Sweden led kings such as Svein Forkbeard and Olaf Tryggvasson to establish the first royal mints, where coins struck in their names served to reinforce their authority. For much of the Viking Age, however, that authority was, to a surprising degree, tempered by the *jarls* and *bóndis*.

The jarl

Forming a small but powerful ruling aristocracy, the *jarls* owned vast tracts of land, much of which was leased to tenant farmers from whom they derived the major part of their wealth by way of revenue and produce. Men living within the principalities of these great chieftains elected them as both

A 14th-century painted wooden panel depicting Olaf Haraldsson, who reigned as king of Norway from 1015 to 1030. In the centre of the panel, the king holds an orb and battleaxe, both strong images of sovereignty. His violent methods of enforcing Christianity eventually led to a revolt by his subjects that culminated in his death at the battle of Stiklestad in 1030. Soon afterwards, he came to be regarded as a martyr and was subsequently enshrined as St Olaf of Norway. (The Restoration Workshop of Nidaros Cathedral)

spiritual and military leaders, and it was the *jarl's* duty to protect these lesser landowners from their enemies; in return, he was entitled to their support in his own disputes and enterprises. It was this ruling caste that held the wealth necessary to retain a personal bodyguard and to commission the building of great halls, earthworks and fine longships, such as those found at Gokstad and Skuldelev.

In times of peace these *jarls*, accompanied by their retainers, would have spent their time overseeing their estates, collecting revenue and supervising the maintenance of their property and ships. Throughout the year, they would also officiate at important religious ceremonies as *godi*, or priests, and would attend the regional public assembly known as the Thing in their capacity as district representative. In times of national conflict, the *jarl* was also responsible for raising the *ledungen*, or levy, which he was expected to lead into battle. Those warriors who sailed, or marched with him, were the *bóndis*.

The bóndi

Forming the backbone of Viking society, these land-owning freemen, or *bóndis*, had the right to bear arms, and whether they were humble smallholders or wealthy men owning substantial farmsteads, they were all entitled to attend the Thing. Here, as we shall see, they could voice their opinions on matters of local concern and even national importance, such as the approval of a king's actions or the suitability of his successor.

In an early scene from the Bayeux Tapestry, an eminent jarl — *in this case, Harold Godwinsson — rides out, hawk on hand. He wears a fine cloak and tunic and is mounted on a spirited horse with a hogged, or braided mane. Accompanied by his retainers, Harold follows his hounds in pursuit of what appear to be two hares. Such a scene would have been a familiar sight to Viking* jarls *in Scandinavia. (The Ancient Art & Architecture Collection Ltd)*

Allegiance to a monarch was by no means automatically conferred by succession, and it behoved a new king to win – and maintain – the respect and loyalty of these proud and outspoken freemen, for in times of war, it was they who constituted the main reservoir of his fighting men. If a king or a *jarl* proved unjust, or his campaigns were dogged by misfortune, the *bóndis* could legitimately discard him and choose a new leader. As freemen and warriors living in a world where personal bravery, skill at arms and an iron will would often carry the day, the more ambitious of them no doubt harboured aspirations of becoming *jarls* or even kings themselves.

The *bóndi*'s first loyalty, however, was to his immediate and extended family. His primary aim in life was the advancement of his family's fame and fortune and, most importantly, the preservation of its honour. Proud, belligerent and quick to take offence, the *bóndi*'s sense of honour was deeply ingrained, and any insult, real or imagined, could result in swift and violent retribution. Inevitably, revenge attacks followed, sparking blood feuds between families that resulted in massacres, ambushes, burnings and duels. As the sagas relate, these feuds were pursued with grim intensity. Until honour had been satisfied, perhaps by the wholesale slaughter of a protagonist's family, or by one side or the other accepting compensation in the form of *wergild* ('man-money'), vengeful fathers would pass on their enmity to their sons.

For much of the time, however, life was not all doom and gloom. The majority of the *bóndis* were self-sufficient, land-owning farmers. On a small farm, the freeman and his family, possibly helped by two or three thralls, would work the land, fell and shape timber, construct and maintain their buildings, operate a smithy, manufacture their own tools and herd and pen their livestock. Any specialized items that were not available locally, such as bog-iron, or those that could not be made at home, such as jewellery, would be obtained through trade or by barter. The wealthier *bóndis* living on extensive farmsteads may well have employed other freemen who were less well off than themselves, along with an appropriate number of thralls to carry out the more strenuous and disagreeable tasks on the farm.

In his spare time, the freeman's recreations would have included hunting, both for food and sport, sword practice, swimming and wrestling. As a rule, children were cared for and valued. In return, they were expected to work hard and learn the skills that their fathers had mastered. Viking poets tell us that the sons of *jarls* and *bóndis* were encouraged to 'shoot arrows, ride on horseback, hunt with hounds, brandish swords and do feats of swimming', outdoor activities that would increase their strength and prepare them for a life in which violence and warfare were almost inevitable. Childhood was brief

One of four carved wooden heads from the Oseberg cart. There are few portraits from the Viking Age that are not highly stylized; this one, however, is totally naturalistic. Alert and well groomed, this is a man of substance who stares directly back at us from over a thousand years ago; he may well be the closest we ever come to the true appearance of a Norseman, or bóndi. (Werner Forman Archive / Viking Ship Museum, Bygdoy)

and there is evidence that on occasion, 12-year-old youngsters accompanied their elders on raiding expeditions.

Running, and a ball game known as *knattleikr*, were popular sports, while fishing for salmon and trout helped fill the larder. Over the long winter nights, a *bóndi* could play board games, such as *hnefatafl*, a northern forerunner of chess, or listen to songs, stories and poems that celebrated the high drama

of conquest, revenge, doomed romance and violent death. For the thrall, however, recreation was an almost non-existent concept.

The thrall

The thrall existed at the very bottom of the social pyramid. That he belonged absolutely to his master is graphically illustrated by the existence of a law that, quite literally, allowed the thrall to be beaten to death by his owner. (For whatever reason, the same law also required that whoever did such a thing must publicly announce the deed on the same day!) It should be pointed out, however, that such an act was generally frowned upon, in much the same way as would be the beating to death of a dog or a horse.

Recognized by their close-cropped hair and rude garments, thralls were put to work on the heaviest of tasks, such as felling trees, digging ditches and spreading dung. Thralls of both sexes worked in the fields, and each day they were also expected to help indoors, fetch and carry water and muck out the pigs and cattle.

Slaves of both sexes were a source of great wealth to the Vikings, and there are accounts of captives being traded in slave markets as far afield as Dublin and Byzantium. Some of these unfortunate souls ended up in the Scandinavian homelands, where they were subjected to a wretched life of back-breaking servitude, their only release being death itself.

That female slaves were often sexually abused by their masters is evident from the writings of Ibn Fadlan, when he encountered the *Rus* on the banks of the Volga in the 10th century. In his often-quoted account of a Viking funeral, the Arab chronicler also describes the fate of a slave girl who was put to death in order to accompany her master on his journey to Valhalla. The burial chamber in the Oseberg ship also contained two corpses, one of which was an elderly female slave, who would tend to the needs of her mistress in the afterlife.

Even a thrall's child became the property of his master, in much the same way as he would own a newborn foal; and when the thrall became old or infirm, he could be disposed of as a lame horse or a dog might be. More often than not, he was even denied a simple burial, his body simply being cast out to the elements.

Not all *bóndis* were such harsh taskmasters, however, and occasionally we see evidence of a hard-working thrall being elevated to the rank of *bryti*, or farm steward. Sometimes, a thrall might even be allowed a degree of free time in which to do extra work on his own behalf, and in time, buy his freedom and emerge from servitude as a freedman.

The institution of slavery was essential to the Viking way of life, and without slave labour it would have been impossible for the *bóndi* to function in the manner expected of him. In the 10th century, for instance, when a Norwegian freeman of modest means was required to leave his holding to serve in the king's levy, the Frostathing Law advised that in his absence the assistance of three thralls was probably enough to keep his farm running efficiently, but that a sizeable estate would require the deployment of 30 or more slaves.

In addition to serving his king, the freeman would usually leave his farm or estate at least once a year in order to further his own ends, perhaps by joining a trading expedition to sell his produce in market towns such as Kaupang or Hedeby, or by voyaging to foreign lands in search of slaves and plunder in his role as Viking. That a man could make such voyages, leaving his

10th-century arm-ring from Denmark. (Werner Forman Archive/National Museum, Copenhagen)

farmstead for months or even years at a time, and return reasonably certain that things would still be running smoothly, was largely due to the robust nature of the women he left behind.

Viking women

On leaving his farm or estate for any length of time, the freeman would make a public show of handing over the keys of the house to his wife, a sign that she was in absolute charge of all things in his absence. Those keys would be added to the bunch of keys that as a married woman she always carried on her person, the most important of which secured the chests containing the family's most precious possessions.

In almost every respect, women in Viking society held equal status with their men. Even when the freeman was at home, it was his wife who had complete authority over all household matters and supervised the thralls and free servants, who would assist her with daily tasks such as spinning, weaving, stitching, brewing drink and preparing food.

One of her most important and time-consuming responsibilities was making clothes for her family. Most garments in the Viking Age were made from woollen cloth, the production of which involved the lengthy process of spinning woollen yarn from raw fleece, dying the yarn and then weaving the finished cloth on a vertical, weighted loom. If flax was available, it could be beaten, spun and woven into linen, which was apparently a popular material for undergarments.

In their spare time, women may also have worked on colourful and intricately patterned braiding, which was tablet-woven and used to trim and decorate clothing. Other handicrafts would have included embroidery and tapestry work, which would have been displayed along the walls of the longhouse. If the family owned a ship or a boat, the women and probably the older members of the family were expected to manufacture sails, a mammoth undertaking that would have consumed months of their time.

There is abundant archaeological evidence that Viking women (and men) were clean, well groomed and particular about their appearance. In the early 10th century, Ibn Fadlan noted that the *Rus* 'were perfect physical specimens' and that their women wore fine jewellery of gold and silver, which reflected the wealth and social status of their husbands. While visiting the thriving town of Hedeby in AD 950, an Arab merchant named Al-Tartushi was also suitably impressed by the Viking women he came across, and while remarking on their beauty, he was astonished by their degree of independence.

From an early age, Viking women were encouraged to be self-reliant and resourceful. An Icelandic law set the earliest marrying age for girls at 12 years, and in outlying farming communities, those marriages would usually be arranged by families. On occasion, however, women were free to choose their own husbands. They were also entitled to own property and inherit wealth in their own right. If necessary, a woman could sue for divorce and when she left, could claim back her dowry and a share of the household goods. If a woman was widowed, she was allowed the dignity of deciding whether to remarry or retain her independence. That these women were imbued with a strong sense of their own worth and could become influential and wealthy figures in Viking society is evident from the quality of their grave goods and the respectful manner in which they were interred. Runestones were also raised in their honour, commemorating good housekeeping skills and mastery of domestic handicrafts, such as sewing and embroidery.

According to the skalds and poets, some Viking women could be forceful to the point of violence, and the sagas are peppered with references to feisty,

Depicting a 10th-century Viking woman, this Danish amulet stands 4 centimetres (1.6 inches) high and is crafted in silver, gilt and neilo. This woman wears a long, decorated dress over what appears to be a pleated chemise, and in her left hand clutches a shawl, which covers her shoulders. Her hair, which is long and carefully combed, is knotted behind her head. (National Museum of Denmark, Copenhagen)

Viking women, 9th–10th centuries. This scene depicts Viking women, wearing typical dress of the period, engaged in a variety of everyday domestic activities. (Angus McBride © Osprey Publishing Ltd)

strong-minded matriarchs who would pursue blood feuds and galvanize their men folk into action. The exploits of one of these women, Freydis, the daughter of Erik the Red, have come down to us in the *Groenlendinga* (or 'Greenlanders'') *Saga*. Freydis and her husband Thorvard, in partnership with two brothers named Helgi and Finnbogi, set sail from Greenland in two ships on a profit-sharing expedition to Vinland. Having arrived safely, Freydis hatched a scheme to take over the ship belonging to the two brothers and tricked her husband into slaying both them and their crew. When Thorvard shrank from killing five women who had accompanied Helgi and Finnbogi, Freydis took up an axe and finished the job herself. While this story is no doubt an extreme example of a Viking woman's behaviour, it is nevertheless a clear indication that some women were not averse to voyaging across

ᚦᚨᚱ ᚢᚨᚱᚢ ᚨᚢᛁ HÖFUM ALLIR EIN LÖG OK EINN SIÐ. ÞAT MUN VERÐA SATT. ER VER SLITUM I SUNDR GÆRR BÆR UNDAR

MENN SKRYDDR AT LÖGIN AT VER MUNUM SITA OK FRBINN SOK ÜEKK ÞOR

Woodcarving showing a meeting of Vikings at the annual Thing, AD 1000, in which a decision is made to embrace Christianity. On the far right a chieftain casts aside his pagan idol. (C M Dixon/The Ancient Art & Architecture Collection Ltd)

dangerous seas on trading expeditions with their husbands and were entitled to share in any profit that was forthcoming. Considering the Viking woman's standing in society, it is surprising to discover that although she was entitled to attend the Thing, she was denied the right to vote.

Viking law – the Thing

The public assembly of land-owning freemen known as the Thing (Assembly) was the cornerstone of democracy and authority in the Viking Age. Each district had its own Thing, and as a rule these open-air assemblies met once or twice a year, although they could be convened more frequently. The basic function of the Thing was to provide an arena where matters of local importance could be debated. Kings were elected, new laws were discussed, disputes over land and property were settled, and violent crime and theft were adjudicated upon. Above the district assemblies was a regional Thing, where the more important decisions taken by the districts would be ratified.

When a man brought his grievance to the Thing, the matter would be considered by the whole assembly, who were then required to reach a unanimous verdict. Once this had been pronounced, it was then incumbent on the winning suitor to seek his own redress, as the Thing was not empowered to enforce its decisions. To defy such a verdict, however, was deemed dishonourable and could have serious consequences, possibly leading to a man being declared an outlaw, which meant that he lost his legal rights, was denied food and shelter and could be slain with impunity. If a plaintiff's grievance involved family honour or revenge for a killing, he could demand that the matter be settled by single combat, which was fought out in front of the gathered assembly. The Vikings obviously found this form of government effective enough and exported it to many of their colonies overseas. Perhaps the best known of these was the Althing, which was founded around AD 930 in Iceland.

The Althing was a national assembly that was held for two weeks every summer at Thingvellir, a dramatic outdoor setting near modern Reykjavik. All Icelandic freemen and their families flocked to the site, and the gathering was as much a social occasion as a formal meeting of parliament. A legislature of 36 Icelandic chieftains would convene to discuss matters of importance; they in turn would elect 36 judges, who would dispense justice when cases came before them. The chairmanship of the Althing fell to the 'Lawspeaker', who was elected every three years and acted as a repository of the law. He presided over the assembly from the 'Law Rock' and each year, as part of his duties, he would recite from memory one-third of the Icelandic laws so that in time, people would become familiar with them. At the conclusion of the Althing, the Icelanders would show their approval of the assembly's decisions by a mass display of weapon shaking, known as the *vápnatak*. By the end of the 11th century, however, Denmark, Norway and Sweden were each dominated by a single, powerful monarch and the authority of the Thing diminished accordingly.

The longhouse

How the farmer, fisherman or town dweller constructed his home was very much dependent on the natural resources to hand. In most parts of Scandinavia there were abundant supplies of timber, and buildings were largely constructed of wood. The exceptions to this rule were the northernmost areas of Norway and the Atlantic colonies, where timber was scarce and stone and turf were employed as building materials. Whatever their location, the basic layout of a Viking dwelling house followed a similar pattern.

A modest longhouse might be 12–15 metres (39–49 feet) in length, although some examples found in Denmark and Norway ran to 50 metres (164 feet) or more. Regardless of its length, the width of the building was restricted by the length of its crossbeams and was rarely in excess of 5 metres (16 feet). The basic framework of these rectangular buildings consisted of four sturdy corner posts, which were sunk directly into the earth. Using wooden trenails, these corner posts were then connected and braced with stout longitudinal and transverse timbers. A pitched roof was carried on a series of crossbeams, which were supported by two rows of vertical posts that ran the length of the building. Walls were formed by filling in the spaces between wall-stakes with wattle-and-daub, or with planks, laid horizontally, one on top of the other. In order to conserve warmth, most longhouses were devoid of windows and had only one door, which was situated in one of the gable ends. The upper sections of both gables were closed with vertical planks, and the roof was thatched or covered with rows of small wooden shingles.

OPPOSITE *Thingvellir, 'Parliament Plains', where the national assembly, Althing, met. (Werner Forman Archive)*

A reproduction of one of the principal beds found on board the Oseberg ship. Such a bed would only have belonged to a wealthy man or woman, who lived in a house large enough to boast a purpose-built bedroom. The headposts terminate in carved animal heads, and inside the frame, a mattress filled with feathers and down would have lain on the horizontal wooden slats. All the beds unearthed at Oseberg could be easily dismantled and may have accompanied their owners whilst travelling. (© Museum of Cultural History, University of Oslo, Norway, photographers Kojan & Krogvold)

Living space may have been divided into three or four 'rooms' that were perhaps screened off by curtains, while broad, sturdy platforms that ran along each side of the building functioned as both beds and sitting areas. Flattened earth served as a floor, and in the centre of the living area was an oblong, stone-lined hearth over which meals were prepared. The hearth not only warmed the building, but also provided a source of light, which was supplemented by the use of oil lamps. Smoke and smells escaped through the door and from small openings at the apex of the gables.

Over the years, the layout of the house would inevitably change, with rooms being added as and when appropriate. In larger houses, the addition of a bedroom for the master and mistress became quite desirable, and in some cases, an entrance hall was added and sections of the main hall were transformed into separate kitchen and weaving areas.

In towns, the homes of craftsmen and merchants would invariably incorporate their workshops, and to the rear, a fenced-off yard where hens, geese and pigs could roam. The yard would also contain a midden for household

IC:COQVI
VR:CARO
ET hIC: MINISTRAVERVN
MINISTRI

rubbish and a cesspit for sewage. In rural areas, the wealthy man's farmhouse was usually surrounded by a cluster of smaller, purpose-built outhouses. These would have included slave quarters, stables, workrooms, storage sheds, byres, barns and a smithy, which stood apart from the other buildings in order to minimize the risk of fire. Some less wealthy farmers were forced to share part of their living quarters with their animals, a somewhat odious arrangement, which at least generated extra warmth in the winter. In both town and country, thralls and the very poor lived in small, squalid huts, some less than 4 square metres (43 square feet), or in wood-lined, sunken pits that were crudely roofed over with thatch.

In this scene from the Bayeux Tapestry, the preparations for a banquet are well underway. Two cooks tend a cauldron that is suspended over a raised firebox, which closely resembles a modern barbecue set. To their right, a man using a pronged fork removes chunks of meat or bread from a stove. (R Sheridan/The Ancient Art & Architecture Collection Ltd)

Food and drink

The longhouse was the centre of Viking daily life, and here meals were prepared and served twice a day, once in the early morning and again in the evening. At dawn, thralls would stoke up the fire in preparation for baking, which was one of the first tasks of the day. Dough was kneaded in long wooden troughs and then baked in clay ovens or directly over the hearth, using long-handled iron pans, similar to those found amongst the Oseberg equipment. Although the wealthy favoured expensive 'white' bread, which was made with wheat, bread was usually made from barley and was eaten while it was still warm, for as it cooled, the

A selection of kitchen utensils from the Oseberg find. The large barrel would have been used to store fish, pork or beef – both salted and smoked. The two oblong troughs on the left were likely used to knead dough and beside them are a knife and a wooden plate, on which meals would have been served. (© Museum of Cultural History, University of Oslo, Norway, photographer Eirik Irgens Johnsen)

unleavened bread soon hardened. Bread would certainly have been offered as part of the morning meal, along with porridge, oatcakes, milk, cold meat and fruit.

When darkness fell, men returned from their tasks and gathered in the longhouse for the main meal of the day. The dishes served from a wealthy farmer's kitchen would have included sausage, fish, eggs, milk, meat, onions, mushrooms, cheese, apples, hazelnuts, strawberries, blackberries and if it was available, honey. Mutton, pork, beef, venison and poultry were boiled or roasted over the hearth on long-handled forks, or on spits. Meat stews, broths and porridge were prepared in large cauldrons made of iron or soapstone, which were suspended above the hearth by iron chains attached to the roof beams, or supported over the fire by an iron tripod, like the example found at Oseberg. Food could be flavoured with wild leeks, garlic, horseradish and a variety of herbs – or with salt, which was prepared by evaporating seawater over a fire.

Meals were served in wooden bowls or on platters, and food was eaten with the fingers or with a wooden spoon, while meat was taken with a knife. Milk from both cattle and goats was drunk with meals and was also churned into butter and cheese, which were stored in large wooden vats. Ale, which was

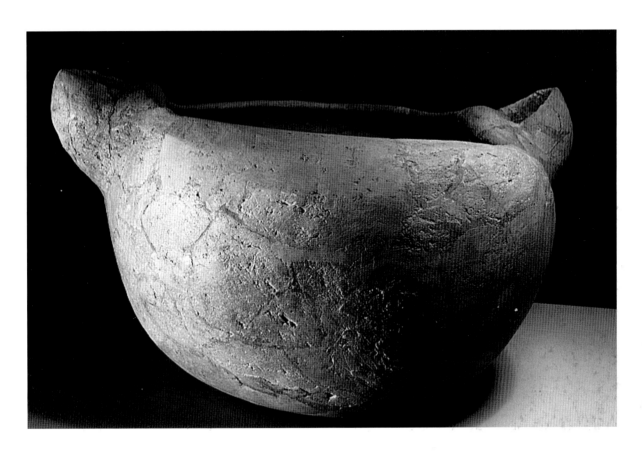

brewed from malted barley and hops, was a firm favourite with all classes and was served up in wooden cups or decorated drinking horns. The wealthy man, however, could savour mead and imported wines from beautifully fashioned glass vessels and silver goblets.

A soapstone bowl from Denmark. Easy to carve, soapstone was one of the major exports from Norway during Viking times and was used as far south as Hedeby, in south-east Denmark. (Werner Forman Archive/National Museum, Copenhagen)

The farm

Due to the vast differences in Scandinavian topography, it is difficult to generalize when discussing the way in which men wrested a living from the land. In the far north and along Norway's western seaboard, survival was dependent on a combination of fishing, hunting and the ownership of sufficient pastureland on which to graze livestock. As a consequence, most farmsteads were remote and scattered far apart. In Denmark and southern Sweden, however, both arable land and rich pasture were plentiful, and archaeological evidence shows that in those areas a large number of farms, both great and small, thrived throughout the Viking Age. In some instances, smaller holdings were grouped together by common interest and operated in the form of collectives and villages.

The farming year began in the spring when ploughing and sowing took place. In its most primitive form, ploughing involved the use of the *ard*, a pointed length of timber usually tipped with iron, which the farmer or thrall guided through the earth while following behind one or two draught animals. Because this rather basic process only incised a single groove, fields would have invariably been cross-ploughed before sowing commenced. In the latter part of the Viking Age, the *ard* was largely replaced by the true plough, complete with iron coulter and mouldshare, which enabled the cutting of deep, parallel furrows such as those uncovered at Lindholm Høje in Denmark.

In the late summer, the whole household, using short scythes and sickles, harvested their crops which would have included barley, oats, rye and, in the more southerly regions, wheat. Grain was left to dry in sheaves on the field and, after threshing, was ground into flour using a quernstone. Vegetables were also cultivated and included peas, onions, cress and cabbages.

During the summer, cattle, sheep and goats were grazed on higher pastures in order to preserve the lower meadows, which yielded the fodder so critical to the survival of cattle and horses throughout the winter months ahead. Before the onset of winter, any weak or infirm animals were slaughtered for meat, which would be preserved by drying, salting or smoking. Their skins would then be tanned and used to manufacture clothing and footwear. During the harshest weather, horses and cattle were sheltered in stables and byres, but goats and sheep were generally expected to survive outdoors.

Although the majority of Viking farms – whether isolated or communal – were run on self-sufficient lines, a crucial part of the farmer's economic well-being was always dependent on having a healthy surplus of marketable goods, such as livestock, grain, milk products and wool, which he could sell at his local town. Many farms would have been situated close to the sea and such journeys were often undertaken by boat. Over land, men travelled on horseback or on foot. Horses were also used as draught animals and pulled both carts and sledges, similar no doubt to those found in the Oseberg burial. In the winter months, sleighs and skis were employed, as were skates made from animal bones.

Religion

The Vikings usually worshipped their gods in the open air – at ancient sites, sacred groves, or on islands – although occasionally people congregated in wooden temples, which contained carved images of the various deities. Sacrifices of animals, crops and sometimes humans were regularly made to the gods, and no matter of importance, such as going to war, building a new

OPPOSITE *A reconstruction of the 12th-century farm complex at Stöng, Iceland. The buildings were constructed from turf squares that were raised on low, substantial stone foundations. The main hall was split into two rooms, and leading from them were two purpose-built offshoots, which probably housed a dairy and room for processing wool. In order to conserve warmth and keep out the damp, the inside walls of the main buildings and the roof were clad in timber, which stood clear of the turf. Nearby were a cattle byre and a smithy, which incorporated a sunken fire pit and a stone anvil. (© Mats Wibe Lund)*

house, or setting out on a long journey, would ever be undertaken without first petitioning the relevant gods for guidance and protection.

The Norsemen viewed their world as a flat disc surrounded by a vast ocean and here, coiled around the earth, dwelt the Midgard Serpent. Supporting the earth was the giant ash tree, Yggdrasill, whose roots stretched from the freezing depths of Hel to Jotunheim, the home of the giants, which lay on the far side of the ocean at the world's end. Beneath the roots of Yggdrasill lay the Well of Fate and Wisdom, which was tended by the Norns, three spirits who wove the threads of destiny. Chained to a rock at the centre of the earth was the ravenous wolf Fenrir, whose jaws stretched across the universe. As the giant wolf struggled against his fetters, trolls and giants schemed against the gods, and the sun and moon crossed the sky, endlessly pursued by wolves.

Mankind dwelt in a realm known as Midgard and lived under the protection of many deities, the most important of which were the Aesir who lived in Asgard, the stronghold of the gods.

First and foremost in this pantheon was Odin, the 'All-Father', the god of kings, knowledge, understanding, magic and poetry. His two ravens, Huginn and Munnin (Thought and Memory), were his constant companions. In his epic quest for knowledge and understanding, he had undergone great suffering, even giving up one of his eyes. Of all the gods, he was the most feared and respected.

Odin was also known as 'the helmeted one', the god of war. Carrying his awesome spear, Gungnir, he rode across the sky on his mighty, eight-legged horse, Sleipnir; the worldly creatures associated with him were the wolf and raven, battlefield carrion that feasted on the corpses of slain warriors. It was the wish of every Viking warrior to die a hero's death on the battlefield and to be chosen by the fierce female spirits known as Valkyries, who would carry the bravest of them to Odin's great 'Hall of the Slain', Valhalla (see 'Motivation and psychology', page 120).

Next to Odin stood his son Thor, the red-haired god of thunder and lightning. Armed with his great hammer, Mjöllnir, Thor's principal task was to guard Asgard and Midgard against the evil Giants of Frost and Fire, whose abiding aim was the destruction of the gods. Kindly, hot-tempered and incredibly strong, he could also be somewhat naïve, and on occasion could be hoodwinked by his more devious enemies. These qualities endeared Thor to the Norsemen, who obviously saw him as a reflection of themselves. Revered by the common man, his widespread popularity is reflected in the number of pendants and amulets that have been unearthed in the form of his famous

hammer. His name was also frequently used as a prefix in place names, such as Thorshavn, Thorburn and Thorness, and in the names Vikings gave themselves: Thorfinn, Thorkil and Thorgrim.

Brooch in the form of the Midgard Serpent. (Werner Forman Archive/Statens Historiska Museet, Stockholm)

While on his adventures, Thor was sometimes accompanied by the god Loki, who represented the forces of mischief and chaos. Known as 'the father of lies', Loki brought about the death of Odin's second son, the beloved Baldr, and his scheming would ultimately bring about Ragnarok and the end of the world.

Living alongside the Aesir were the Vanir, a divine race to which Frey and his sister Freyja, the goddess of earth and nature, belonged. These two deities were associated with fertility, birth, pleasure and prosperity. It was Frey who was toasted at weddings, and in the spring men sought his blessing when crops were planted.

An impression of Valhalla from an 8th-century picture stone from Tjängvide, Gotland. Riding his great steed Sleipnir, Odin welcomes two fallen warriors to his 'Hall of the Slain', possibly represented by the building with the curved roof at upper left. On Odin's left, a Valkyrie offers what could be a horn of ale, or mead, to the fallen heroes. The animal behind her may be a dog, or one of Odin's wolves. (Werner Forman Archive/Statens Historiska Museet, Stockholm)

As with mortal men, however, even the gods could not escape death. As Ragnarok dawns, the Giants, in league with Loki, begin their march on Asgard. The massive wolf Fenrir breaks free from his chains, and the Midgard Serpent, spewing venom, rises from the sea. As the world tree Yggdrasill trembles, Heimdal, the watchman of Asgard, blows his horn and the gods, along with the slain heroes of Valhalla, arm themselves for the final battle. Frey is first to die, slain by the Fire Giant, Surt; Odin spears Fenrir, who then devours him and is in turn slaughtered by Odin's son, Vidar; Thor engages the terrifying Midgard Serpent and each is the death of the other. Heimdal and the treacherous Loki destroy one another, stars fall from the sky, the sun is extinguished and the earth is swallowed by the sea.

In the wake of this cosmic destruction, however, Baldr is resurrected, and the sons of Odin and Thor, along with a mortal man and woman, live to see

a new order arise. With it comes the possibility of a new All-Father, which some interpret as the coming of Christianity.

The Norsemen listened to poems and legends about the gods since childhood and strove to emulate their virtues and achievements in their own daily lives. Advice from Odin on a man's behaviour was forthcoming in the *Hávamál*, the 'Sayings of the High One', much of which is as relevant today as it was a thousand years ago:

Only a fool lies awake all night and broods over his problems. When morning comes, he is worn out and his troubles the same as before.

A big gift is not necessary. Esteem can often be bought on the cheap. With half a loaf and a tilted bottle, I have gained a companion.

Praise no day until evening, no wife before her cremation, no sword till tested, no maid before marriage, no ice till crossed, no ale till it's drunk.

Cattle die, kinsfolk die, we ourselves must die. One thing I know will never die – the dead man's reputation.

THE VIKINGS ABROAD
The Vikings in England: 9th–10th centuries

After the initial Viking attacks on England at the end of the 8th century there followed a period of relative calm, which was finally shattered some 40 years later when, in 835, the *Anglo-Saxon Chronicle* records that 'heathen men ravaged Sheppey'. Thereafter, for the rest of the century, hardly a year goes by without the *Chronicle* recording a Viking incursion somewhere in the country. At first these expeditions were no more than predatory raids launched during the summer months in search of booty and slaves, with no attempt being made at permanent settlement. In 850/851, however, there were signs of a change in strategy: the *Chronicle* reports under that year that 'for the first time, the heathen stayed through the winter', on the Isle of Thanet. In 855/856 a Viking host again 'stayed for the entire winter', this time on the Isle of Sheppey; in 864/865 Vikings again wintered on Thanet; and finally, in 865/866, a 'great fleet of pagans', having arrived from the Continent, wintered in East Anglia. This time the Vikings had come to stay.

The 'great fleet' that arrived in 865 included amongst its leaders several sons of the celebrated Danish king, Ragnar Lodbrok ('Hairy-breeches'), who was regarded in the North as the very epitome of a true Viking. The sons in question were Ivar the Boneless, Halfdan, and Ubbi or Hubba, and *Ragnar's Saga* would have it that their attack was launched purely to avenge the alleged death in

Developments in Scandinavian shipbuilding in the 8th century led to the appearance of the longship — a key tool for Viking expansion in England and beyond. This is one of the ornamental gilt copper or bronze vanes (vedrviti) that the sagas record to have been carried on the prows of many Viking longships as a sign of importance. Four examples have survived as wind-vanes on church steeples: this one comes from Söderala, Hälsingland, Sweden, and likely dates to the 10th century. Such vanes remained in use for as long as Viking-style longships did, and probably found their way on to church steeples as a result of the traditional practice of stowing the sails and other movable items of levy ships' equipment in local churches. (© Gabriel Hildebrand/The Museum of National Antiquities, Stockholm, Sweden)

the 850s of their father at the hands of King Aella of Northumbria, who was supposed to have had him cast into a snake-pit after capturing him in battle. Despite the fact that Aella had only come to power in 866 and Ragnar had in reality probably been killed by a Norse king in Ireland, it is undeniable that, after they had spent a year looting and gathering reinforcements in East Anglia, Ragnar's sons attacked and took York at the end of 867; and the next year captured and ritually executed Aella, subsequently overrunning much of Northumbria and eastern Mercia (868). In 869, Ivar led part of the host back to East Anglia, where he defeated and captured King Edmund who, like Aella, was executed. (Though Edmund was also seemingly shot through with arrows, both kings were actually killed by being subjected to the gruesome 'blood-eagle' torture, in which the living victim had a number of ribs chopped away from his spine; his lungs were pulled out through these massive wounds to lie pulsing on his back like red wings until he died.) Ivar subsequently disappears from the story (he seems to have removed to Ireland and conquered Dublin, where he probably died in 873); and Halfdan became the host's chief leader in his stead, being the foremost of the seven Viking commanders recorded at the battle of Ashdown in 871, of whom the other six (a king and five *jarls*) were all killed in this celebrated Saxon victory. The English success was short-lived, however: a series of defeats followed at Basing, Meretun, Reading and Wilton, by the end of which King Alfred of Wessex was obliged to sue for peace, not least because a new army of Vikings, referred to as the 'summer army', had now arrived from the Continent to reinforce Halfdan, and had participated in the Saxon defeat at Wilton.

For the next few years the Vikings concentrated on securing their conquests in eastern and northern England. They briefly set up puppet kings in both Northumbria and Mercia (the last Saxon king of the latter fled in 874) before distributing these kingdoms among themselves in 876 and 877, respectively. Halfdan then followed in the footsteps of his brother Ivar, sailing to Ireland in a bid to secure for himself the kingdom of Dublin, only to be defeated and killed by Norwegian Vikings in the battle of Strangford Lough (877).

This resulted in a certain Guthrum – who, with two other kings named Oskytel and Anwend, had commanded the 'summer army' of 871 (now based in Cambridge) – becoming the chief captain of the Danish host in England. In 878 Guthrum came within an ace of extinguishing the last independent Saxon kingdom, as the *Anglo-Saxon Chronicle* reports:

> the host went secretly in midwinter … and rode over Wessex and occupied it, and drove a great part of its inhabitants overseas, and reduced the greater part of the rest to submission, except Alfred the king; and he with a small company moved under difficulties through woods and into inaccessible places in marshes.

With Alfred still free, however, there was no chance for permanent Viking occupation. He struck out at the Viking invaders from a fortress he had established at Athelney – 'surrounded by swampy, impassable and extensive marshland and groundwater on every side' and inaccessible except by boat – and soon afterwards, rallying the men of Somerset, Wiltshire and Hampshire, routed Guthrum at the battle of Edington (Ethandun). As a result of this defeat Guthrum and the other Viking leaders were obliged to hand over hostages, embrace Christianity and leave Wessex.

A somewhat later peace treaty drawn up between Alfred and Guthrum in 886 effectively established the area of Danish occupation that was later (by the 11th century) to become known as the Danelaw, comprising East Anglia and the 'Five Boroughs' of Derby, Leicester, Lincoln, Nottingham and Stamford.

Evidence of the extent of Scandinavian settlement in this area can still be seen today in the number of place-names ending in -*thorpe* ('village'), -*thwaite* ('meadow') and -*by* ('farmstead').

The very same year another Viking host descended on England, but after wintering at Fulham understandably withdrew to the Continent, where they carved a trail of mayhem and destruction for more than a decade. In 892, however, following a defeat the previous year at the hands of Arnulf, king of Eastern Francia, this 'Great Army' returned to England, bringing with it from Boulogne its own horses. Several years of spasmodic fighting ensued throughout the length and breadth of Alfred's kingdom; but in the summer of 896, 'the Viking army dispersed, some into East Anglia, some into Northumbria, and those who were without property got ships for themselves and went south across the sea to the Seine'. The fact that the last group sailed in just five ships, and therefore numbered no more than 350–400 men at most, would tend to confirm the view of various modern authorities that this so-called 'Great Army' may have consisted of no more than 1,000 men in all; some even believe it may have comprised just 500 men.

Even after the 'Great Army' had disbanded, the resident Vikings of East Anglia and Northumbria continued to harass Wessex by land and sea. However, King Alfred, who died in 899, had left to his successors a strong, well-organized military establishment both on land and at sea with which Edward the Elder (899–925) and Athelstan (925–940) were able to reconquer the Danelaw. Northumbria held out somewhat longer, partly due to the influx of a new wave of Viking invaders – this time Norsemen from Ireland, who captured York from the Danes in 919, and established their own dynasties there which were accepted by Scandinavian settlers and Northumbrian Saxons alike. At one time or another, they also ruled over the Norse settlements of Ireland, the Western Isles and the Orkneys, as well as the Five Boroughs. Nevertheless, King Rognvald of York acknowledged South Saxon suzerainty as early as 920, as did King Sihtric in 926; and in 927 Athelstan marched on York and evicted Sihtric's son and successor Olaf, and his brother, Olaf's mentor and regent, Guthfrith. However, the latter's own son, another Olaf, recaptured York before the end of 939 and the very next year received the Five Boroughs by treaty. He was succeeded as king of York by his less vigorous cousin Olaf Sihtricsson (who had been thrown out in 927), from whom the South Saxons were able to retake the Five Boroughs in a single decisive campaign in 942, Olaf himself being expelled in 944.

Olaf made at least one comeback, in 949–952, but the dubious distinction of being the last Viking king of York undoubtedly belongs to a son of King Harald Fairhair of Norway, the celebrated Erik Bloodaxe, who has been

OPPOSITE *9th- and 10th-century Norwegian weapons: a Gokstad shield, the Gjermundbu helmet, and swords, spearheads and axeheads from various sites.* (© *Museum of Cultural History, University of Oslo, Norway, photographer Ernst Schwitters*)

described as 'the most famous Viking of them all'. He reigned in Northumbria twice, in 947–948 and 952–954. The *Anglo-Saxon Chronicle* states simply that in 954 'the Northumbrians drove Erik out' and that King Eadred of England thereby succeeded to the kingdom; but later Icelandic sagas, deriving their information from a lost 10th-century Northumbrian chronicle, give a fuller account. According to them Erik was confronted at a place called Stainmore by 'King Olaf, a tributary king of King Edmund [sic]':

> [King Olaf] had gathered an innumerable mass of people, with whom he marched against King Erik. A dreadful battle ensued, in which many Englishmen fell; but for each one that fell there came three in his place from the country round about, and

Viking sword hilt from the River Lea, Hertfordshire. (© Copyright the Trustees of the British Museum, MME 1915,0504.1)

when evening came on the loss of men turned against the Northmen and many were killed. Towards the end of the day, King Erik and five kings with him fell. Three of them were Guttorm, Ivar and Harek [the last-named being one of his sons]; the others being Sigurd and Ragnvald [the latter one of his brothers] and with them died the two sons of Turf-Einar [the Earl of Orkney], Arnkel and Erlend.

A much later English chronicle, probably working from the same lost account, would have it that Erik was in fact defeated and killed by a certain Maccus (Magnus), son of Olaf, rather than by Olaf himself, and it is likely – since his army comprised Englishmen – that the sagas' 'Olaf' is in fact an error for Oswulf, who was the Saxon earl of Bamburgh.

Hilt of a sword found in Ballinderry (Westmeath), Ireland. The patterning on the hilt and pommel is of silver. (This image is reproduced with the kind permission of the National Museum of Ireland)

Either way, Erik was dead and the Viking kingdom of York at an end. 'From that time to the present,' wrote John of Wallingford, 'Northumbria has been grieving for want of a king of its own, and for the liberty they once enjoyed.'

The Vikings in Ireland: the battle of Clontarf

Though it has been suggested that a fleet that raided the Hebrides and northern Ireland in 617 may actually have been Scandinavian, the first positively recorded Viking raid on Ireland dates to 795, when the island of Reachrainn (often identified with Lambey Island near Dublin, but more probably Rathlin Island, five miles north-east of the Irish mainland) was plundered and two monasteries on the west coast were sacked. At first no more than hit-and-run affairs executed by small forces, these raids intensified after 830; and colonization commenced *c.* 840 with the arrival of a certain Turgesius, or Turgeis – a semi-legendary character who, according to the Irish chroniclers, made himself 'King of all the Foreigners in Erin'. Dublin was established at about this time when a *longphort* was constructed at a ford on the River Liffey, the Vikings first wintering there in 841–842. Before long similar Viking encampments and settlements had sprung up along much of Ireland's coastline and, further inland, along the courses of its navigable waterways – Cork, Limerick, Waterford, Wexford and Wicklow being the major examples (though most of these only became important in the 10th century). With the exception of just one brief period in 902–919, Dublin was thereafter the seat of Viking power in Ireland under its own self-appointed kings.

One inevitable result of settling down in Ireland was that the Viking communities (mostly of Norsemen) soon found themselves being drawn into the unstable Irish political scene, where petty kings of minor kingdoms were almost continually at war with one another. Alliances between Vikings and Irishmen were, therefore, not uncommon after the mid-9th century, the Dublin Vikings even becoming traditional allies of the kings of Leinster. Indeed, it was this last alliance that in 1014 led to one of the most celebrated battles in Viking and Irish history, when the king of Dublin supported Máelmórdha of Leinster in his rebellion against the high king, Brian Boru. The battle, of course, was Clontarf.

Brian Boru, a dynamic and ambitious chieftain, was one of the few high kings of the medieval period who could with any justification claim to be king of Ireland in more than just name – an achievement that did not endear him to the country's many and fiercely independent petty dynasts. At the very end of the 10th century, in the closing months of 999, Máelmórdha of Leinster and King Sigtrygg Silkybeard of Dublin rose in revolt against Brian, who

Viking battleaxes and spears from the Thames at London Bridge, c. 840–c. 1020. These weapons were possibly left after a battle, or alternatively were thrown into the river as an offering to the gods. (HIP / Museum of London / Topfoto)

marched to meet them in the foothills of the Wicklow Mountains. He inflicted a crushing defeat on their combined forces at Glenn Máma, Máelmórdha only escaping the carnage by taking refuge in a yew tree. Although he and Sigtrygg were subsequently reinstated in their kingdoms by the magnanimous victor, their humiliation at Brian's hands was a festering wound which, according to one account, was tactlessly reopened by Brian's hot-headed son Murchad in 1012. The story would have it that Murchad, beaten in a game of chess as a result of Máelmórdha giving advice to his opponent, cursed the king of Leinster and observed that his advice was not always so fruitful: 'How wonderfully you advised the Norsemen that day they were smashed by us at Glenn Máma!' Deeply offended, Máelmórdha replied, 'I'll advise them again, but this time the outcome will be different,' to which Murchad retorted, 'Be sure to have a yew tree ready!'

Máelmórdha departed angrily from Brian's court, rallied his chieftains, and urged rebellion among the northern kings; by 1013 war had broken out in several quarters. However, Murchad soon had Máelmórdha on the run, and in the late summer he was obliged to take refuge with Sigtrygg in fortified Dublin. Here they were invested by Murchad and Brian until Christmas, when Brian's Munster army broke camp and dispersed for the winter. Making the most of this unexpected respite, Sigtrygg took ship for the north, sailing to the courts of the Viking-held Western Isles in search of allies. According to the *Annals of Innisfallen*, he subsequently received troops from the *Gaill* or 'Foreigners' of the whole Western world, various accounts referring to Viking reinforcements arriving from the Hebrides, Caithness, Kintyre, Argyll, Norway and – more improbably – France, Flanders, Frisia and even Russia. Certainly Earl Sigurd the Stout of Orkney is known to have come to Sigtrygg's support, as did a certain Brodir of Man with 20 ships (though his partner Ospak, with another ten ships, joined Brian).

In the spring of 1014, all these forces assembled outside Dublin, where towards the end of April the high king confronted them with an army estimated at some 20,000 men drawn from Munster, the *Mide* ('Midlands') and southern Connacht. On 23 April – Good Friday – both sides drew up for battle on the plain of Clontarf.

There have been various attempts at establishing the dispositions of the two armies, few of them wholly convincing. However, scholars seem to fundamentally agree that the Vikings and their Leinster allies, drawn up in five or seven divisions, spread themselves too thin in an effort to defend not only their line of retreat back into Dublin across a bridge over the Liffey, but also, on the opposite flank, to cover the ships of the foreign Vikings anchored in Dublin Bay. *Njal's Saga* puts Brodir on one flank, King Sigtrygg on the other, and Earl Sigurd in the centre, but makes no mention of Máelmórdha or his Leinstermen despite the fact that they must have outnumbered the Viking element by at least two to one. It is in error, too, in assigning Sigtrygg a battlefield role, since he remained in Dublin throughout the battle, his brother Dubhgall commanding the Dublin contingent in his place. Probably the foreign Vikings under Sigurd and Brodir were mostly on the left flank in order to protect their ships, while the Dubliners guarded the bridge on the right, and Máelmórdha held the high ground commanding the centre of the line. The disposition of Brian's forces is even more problematic. We know that their right flank was secured on the River Liffey, and their left on the parallel River Tolka. *Njal's Saga* says that the high king, now 73 years old, 'did not wish to wield weapons on Good Friday; so a wall of shields was formed round him and his army was drawn up in front of it'. Murchad was therefore in command, along

These Vikings display Viking costume typical of the 9th–10th centuries. Note the variation in tunics, helmets and breeches. Swords, axes, spears and shields comprised the basic armament. (Angus McBride © Osprey Publishing Ltd)

with his cousin Conaing and 15-year-old son Toirdelbach; the saga also claims that Brian's youngest son Tadg was present. The 12th-century *War of the Gaedhil with the Gaill* – which says that Brian stayed at prayer in his tent in Tomar's Wood – describes the Irish formation as a phalanx of men so tightly packed together that 'a four-horsed chariot could run from one end to the other of the line on their heads, so compact were they'; but it also mentions individual *battals*, or divisions, and three distinct lines.

'The armies clashed, and there was bitter fighting', says *Njal's Saga*. In the centre of the line Máelmórdha led a downhill charge that drove deep into Murchad's ranks, but his Viking allies on either flank fared less well. After heavy fighting, Murchad's predominance in numbers – still apparent despite the withdrawal of the forces of *Mide* before the battle – began to prevail. The Leinstermen, having advanced too far unsupported, were driven back in disarray, as were the Vikings. The Dubliners on the right, falling back towards the town, were pursued so closely that allegedly only 20 men, or according to one version only nine, actually reached the fortress alive. The Viking left flank meanwhile rallied and the Leinstermen fell back on it; but they were now virtually encircled on both left and right by Murchad's victorious Munstermen. They had no choice but to retreat towards the sea, from which there was little hope of escape since high tide had put the Vikings' ships beyond reach of all but the strongest swimmers. Inevitably, therefore, a great many met their death by drowning.

However, despite the fact that some 12 hours of solid fighting had now elapsed, this was not quite the end of the battle. In their desperation some Vikings – Brodir among them – actually managed to hack through Murchad's army and reach the high king's encampment behind the Irish lines. *Njal's Saga* details the events:

> Brodir could see that King Brian's forces were pursuing the fugitives ... and that there were only a few men left to man the wall of shields. He ran from the woods and burst through the shield-wall and hacked at the king. The boy Tadg threw up an arm to protect Brian, but the sword cut off the arm and the king's head ... Then Brodir shouted, 'Let the word go out that Brodir has felled Brian.'

However, he had little time to enjoy his triumph, since he and his companions were surrounded and taken captive by the high king's bodyguards, and subsequently executed.

The *War of the Gaedhil with the Gaill* gives the losses of the Viking–Leinster allies as 2,500 Norsemen and 3,100 Irishmen – 5,600 in all. Other accounts

give a total of 6,000, or 6,000 foreigners; the highest believable estimate, in the *Leabhar Oiris*, claims 6,700 Viking dead and 1,100 Leinstermen, while several say that the Viking losses numbered not fewer than 3,000 men, including the 1,000 in mail corselets who had seemingly been commanded by Brodir. In addition, virtually all of their leaders had been killed, including Earl Sigurd, Brodir, Dubhgall and Máelmórdha: it was claimed that no Viking of rank present on the battlefield was left alive at the end of the day. Nevertheless, it was a somewhat Pyrrhic victory — not only was the high king dead, but so too

The emperor's bodyguards in this Byzantine manuscript, Madrid Skylitzes, *are made up of foreigners, including Franks, Russians, Germans and Vikings. (Werner Forman Archive/Biblioteca Nacional, Madrid)*

was his son, Murchad (he died early the next morning of a mortal wound), his grandson, Toirdelbach, who drowned in the pursuit and his nephew, Conaing. At least seven other kings and 1,600 nobles had also been killed. One account puts the losses of the men of Munster and Connacht at 4,000 in all.

Though significant in many respects, the battle of Clontarf was not as decisive as we are often led to believe. It did not mark the end of Scandinavian power in Ireland – that had already begun to wane in the mid-10th century – and King Sigtrygg continued to rule undisturbed in Dublin for another 20 years. However, other than in occasional piratical forays (such as Magnus Barelegs's campaign of 1101), it would be a century and a half before a foreign Scandinavian army again fought on Irish soil.

The Vikings in the East: the Varangian Guard

Although they had been trading in the eastern Baltic since at least the 7th century, the first eastward Viking raid on record took place at the relatively late date of 852, when a Swedish host descended on the city of Novgorod and exacted a huge Danegeld from its citizens. Even thereafter Vikings in the East – always mainly Swedes – tended to be settlers and traders rather than pirates; they were nevertheless quick to establish themselves as rulers over the native Slavic population, who called them *Rus* (whence 'Russia'). By 858, they had established themselves in Kiev, from where, just two years later, they launched a daring – albeit unsuccessful – attack on Constantinople (Miklagäard, 'The Great Town', as they called it) by sailing their ships down the Dnieper and across the Black Sea. Further major campaigns against the Byzantine Empire

Eastern Vikings, 10th–11th centuries. Viking traders and warriors travelling in the East inevitably adopted, and brought back with them to Scandinavia, assorted Slavic and Central Asian modes of dress and weapons, as these figures clearly testify. The figure on the right is a Rus warrior. The figure on the left has equipment displaying considerable Central Asian influence, including a Magyar-style horse harness. The background figures are Varangian Guardsmen of the 11th century, displaying the two attributes for which they were justly famous – their axes and their drinking. (Angus McBride © Osprey Publishing Ltd)

were to follow in 907, 941 and 944, by which time the *Rus* had already begun to be assimilated by their Slavic subjects and can no longer truly be regarded as Vikings; indeed, even in the mid-9th century the Arabic geographer Ibn Khordadbah described the *Rus* as a 'kind of Slav'.

Real Vikings, referred to by the *Rus*, Arabs and Byzantines alike as 'Varangians', nevertheless continued to feature in Russian history, sizeable bands of them being hired as mercenaries by successive Kievan and Novgorodian princes – a practice that continued well into the 11th century, the last reference to Viking mercenaries in Russia dating to 1043. Many such Vikings, after a spell in Russia, went on to Constantinople and joined the Byzantine army, in which 700 of them are recorded as early as 911. Thereafter, references to Vikings in Byzantine employ are frequent: seven ships crewed by 415 Vikings from Russia accompanied a Byzantine expedition to Italy in 935; six ships and 629 men sailed on a similar expedition to Crete in 949; *Rus* or Viking troops are recorded fighting the Arabs in 955 and taking part in a campaign in Sicily in 968. Twenty years later, in 988, Vladimir of Kiev sent as many as 6,000 Vikings to the assistance of Emperor Basil II, and it was from among these that the celebrated Varangian Guard was subsequently established.

The foundation of the Varangian Guard – or the 'Axe-bearing Guard' as it was often termed in Byzantine sources – resulted from Basil II's distrust of his native Byzantine guardsmen. His contrasting confidence in Vladimir's Russian Vikings probably resulted from familiarity with the descriptions of Arab travellers, who recorded how the loyalty of these *Rus* to their own king was such that they were prepared to 'die with him and let themselves be killed for him'. This confidence was not misplaced, since Anna Comnena would later write of 11th-century Varangian Guardsmen that 'they regard loyalty to the emperors and the protection of their persons as a family tradition, a kind of sacred trust and inheritance handed down from generation to generation; this allegiance they preserve inviolate and will never brook the slightest hint of betrayal.' Scandinavians – whether from Sweden, Norway, Denmark or Iceland – were therefore always welcome at the Byzantine court, and the Icelandic sagas and surviving runic inscriptions alike contain innumerable references to men who at one time or another served in the Varangian Guard. Even Harald Hardrada, future king of Norway, became an officer in the Guard.

The Varangian Guard continued to be composed principally of Scandinavians for about a century and a half after its foundation; but after the Norman Conquest of England in 1066, a great many Anglo-Saxon émigrés also began to be incorporated into its ranks. First recorded in Byzantine employ in the 1070s and 1080s, when they were seemingly brigaded separately from the

This is the celebrated Piraeus Lion, a 12-foot-tall (3.7 metres) white marble statue that used to stand in the Greek harbour of Piraeus near Athens. Upon its shoulders are the weathered and vandalized remains of two now illegible runic inscriptions relating to Vikings in the service of the Byzantine emperor. Some have tried to find in them references to Harald Hardrada; but the style of the inscriptions is clearly Swedish rather than Norwegian, and they probably date to c. 1000 and the second half of the 11th century. (Ian Heath)

Scandinavians, these English guardsmen steadily increased in numbers during the 12th century until, by *c.* 1180, the Byzantine chronicler Cinnamus was able to state quite specifically that the Varangian Guard was composed of men 'of British race'. Even so, *Sverri's Saga* records that as late as 1195 the emperor despatched envoys to the kings of Norway, Sweden and Denmark, requesting 1,200 men for service in the Guard; while Villehardouin's chronicle of the Fourth Crusade of 1202–04 repeatedly refers to Danish, as well as English, guardsmen. By this late date, however, they were undoubtedly in the minority, and later 13th-century sources invariably refer to the Varangians as being *Englinoi* ('Englishmen'). The Viking adventure in the East was over.

The Vikings in England: 11th century

While Viking power had been waning in Ireland and the East, in England it had undergone an unexpected revival following the accession in 978 of the weak and indecisive King Ethelred *Unraed* ('the poorly counselled'), remembered by posterity as Ethelred the Unready. Piratical raids resumed in 980 and gradually increased in size and severity over the next 30 years, despite the frequent payment of Danegeld in an attempt to buy the raiders off: 10,000lbs (4,536kg) of silver were paid out thus in 991, and 16,000lbs (7,257kg) in 994, thereafter increasing with each renewed demand to as much as 48,000lbs (21,773kg) by 1012. Encouraged by the lure of such massive sums of money, Danish Vikings raided England almost every year between

Later Viking warrior, 10th–11th centuries. By this period the character of fighting men of middle rank had undergone remarkable changes. The hersir had ceased to be an independent figure in the Norse states, legitimized by wealth, power and ancestry. Instead he was now a representative of royal authority. Both the local leader and the retained bodyguard could be expected to appear for war equipped like this figure. (Gerry Embleton © Osprey Publishing Ltd)

997 and 1014; and the country's ill-led military establishment weakened and collapsed beneath the systematic onslaught that was masterminded by King Swein Forkbeard, king of Denmark *c.* 984–1014. Eventually, in 1013, the people of Northumbria and East Anglia acknowledged Swein as their sovereign, thereby establishing a line of Viking kings of England which comprised Swein (1013–14); his son Cnut (1016–35), and the latter's own sons Harald Harefoot (1035–40) and Harthacnut (1040–42). Though this line died out with Harthacnut, its claim to the English throne was later revived by the Norwegian king Harald Sigurdsson, who had inherited it from his nephew Magnus the Good, king of Denmark and Norway 1042–47.

Harald Sigurdsson, posthumously nicknamed *Hardradi* ('the Ruthless'), had led a checkered and varied career typical of many Viking chieftains. The son of a petty Norwegian king ruling the Ringerike district, he had fought in support of his half-brother King Olaf Haraldsson (St Olaf) at the battle of Stiklestad in 1030, where the latter was killed. He thereafter fled east to the court of King Jaroslav of Russia. After staying there for several years, during which time he fought against the Poles, he set off to Constantinople 'with a large following' and was enrolled into the celebrated Varangian Guard. He fought against the Arabs in Anatolia and Sicily under Georgios Maniakes, and under other Byzantine generals in southern Italy and Bulgaria, before being imprisoned in Constantinople for apparent misappropriation of imperial booty taken in the course of these expeditions. He appears to have escaped during a popular rising against the Emperor Michael Calaphates in 1042, and thereafter returned to Scandinavia via Russia. Reaching Denmark, he assisted Svein Ulfsson in his struggle against Harald's nephew, King Magnus, for the succession to the Danish throne; but went over to Magnus in 1045 in exchange for a half-share in the kingdom of Norway, succeeding to the other half on Magnus's death in 1047.

He was 51 years old when, in 1066, Tostig, the exiled earl of Northumbria and brother of King Harold Godwinsson of England, arrived in Norway in search of military support to regain his lost earldom. Hardrada had had designs on the English throne at least since the 1050s, and needed little encouragement from Tostig. *King Harald's Saga* says that 'the earl and the king talked together often and at length; and finally they came to the decision to invade England that summer'. A massive fleet was assembled in the south of Norway: the saga puts it at 240 ships ('apart from supply-ships and smaller craft'), and the *Anglo-Saxon Chronicle* puts it at 300, carrying 'a great pirate host' that has been estimated by modern authorities as numbering at least 9,000–10,000 men, and possibly as many as 18,000. This fleet was

joined off the Orkneys by Earl Tostig with 12 vessels of his own, crewed by his household troops and Flemish pirates; from there the whole allied host sailed down to the Humber estuary, plundering as it went, and then upriver as far as Riccall, about 10 miles south of York. Here the Norsemen disembarked to confront the Saxon army that had marched against them from York under the command of Earl Morkere of Northumbria and Earl Edwin of Mercia. *King Harald's Saga* details the attack:

King Harald went ashore and drew up his army. One flank reached down to the river and the other stretched inland along the line of a ditch, where there was a deep and broad morass, full of water. The earls led their army slowly down along the river in close formation. King Harald's banner was near the river, where his line was thickest, but the thinnest part was along the line of the ditch, where his least reliable men were placed. When the earls advanced along the ditch the Norsemen there gave way and the English followed with Morkere's banner in the van, thinking that the Norsemen would flee.

When King Harald saw that the English array was advancing down the ditch and was opposite him, he ordered the attack to be sounded and urged his men forward. Ordering his banner Landwaster to be carried in front of him, he made

Viking made good. King Cnut with his wife Ymma Aelgyfu (Ethelred the Unready's widow) presenting a gold cross to the New Minster at Winchester. From the frontispiece of the Liber Vitae, the Register of New Minster and Hyde Abbey, c. 1020–30. (HIP/The British Library/Topfoto)

such a severe onslaught that everything gave way before him; and there was a great loss among the men of the earls, and they soon broke in flight, some fleeing upriver and others downriver, but most fled into the marsh, which became so filled up with their dead that the Norsemen could pursue them dry-shod.

So ended the battle of Fulford, fought on Wednesday 20 September. The longest version of the *Anglo-Saxon Chronicle* contains only a brief mention of this engagement, claiming that after the earls' army had 'made great slaughter' of the Vikings, 'a great number of the English were either slain or drowned and dispersed in flight, and the Norsemen had possession of the place of slaughter'.

York offered no further resistance to the Vikings, but opened negotiations with Harald, agreeing to accept him as king and to hand over hostages. It was in order to accept these hostages that Harald encamped at Stamford Bridge, seven miles east of York, on 24 September, having left as much as a third of his army with the fleet at Riccall under the command of Eystein Orri, 'the noblest of all the lendermen [landed men, i.e. nobles]'. The rest of the army was ill equipped for what was to follow. *King Harald's Saga* describes how, because the weather was hot and sunny, 'they left their armour behind and went ashore with only their shields, helmets and spears, and girt with swords. A number also had bows and arrows, and all were very carefree.' It must therefore have come as a terrible shock to see not hostages approaching the next day, but 'a large force coming towards them. They could see a cloud of dust raised as from horses' hooves, and under it the gleam of handsome shields and white coats-of-mail.' It was another Saxon army, this time led by King Harold Godwinsson himself, and including in its ranks the famed English Huscarls, each of whom one of Hardrada's own marshals had described as 'worth any two of the best men in King Harald's army'. The saga would have it that, in one last attempt to save his errant brother, Harold called for a parley and offered Tostig a third of his kingdom if he would only join him. It was Tostig's enquiry as to what compensation Hardrada would then receive for his trouble that prompted the now-famous reply, 'Seven feet of English soil, or as much more as he is taller than other men.'

Snorri Sturlusson's description of the ensuing battle in *King Harald's Saga*, the only detailed one we have, is suspect on several counts, not least of which is that he appears to have confused aspects of it with the battle of Hastings. However, it seems likely that when the English army appeared, the Norwegians were probably scattered on both sides of the River Derwent, which explains the celebrated incident recorded in the *Anglo-Saxon Chronicle* where 'one Norwegian stood firm against the [advancing] English forces, so that they could not cross the bridge nor clinch victory. An Englishman shot at him with an arrow but to

OPPOSITE *Viking warriors, 12th century. These three figures bear witness to the gradual evolution of Scandinavian military equipment in the course of the 12th century, which brought it into line with that now employed throughout mainland Europe. It can be seen that conventional long 'kite' shields had by now replaced the old traditional round type; and that mail armour was in general use amongst the new knightly warrior caste that had begun to evolve under Western influence. (Angus McBride © Osprey Publishing Ltd)*

Illustration from the collection of Icelandic sagas, the Flateyjarbok. *This illumination from* King Olaf Tryggvasson's Saga *depicts some of his legendary exploits — the killing of a wild boar and a sea ogress. Though this tale has mythical elements, sagas are an invaluable source of Viking life and history. (Werner Forman Archive / Stofnun Arna Magnussonar a Islandi, Reykjavik, Iceland)*

no avail, and another went under the bridge and stabbed him [through a gap in it] under his mail corselet.' This delay, however, had enabled the outnumbered Norsemen to draw up their main body on the further bank, arranging it in a circle bristling with spears and 'with shields overlapping in front and above', against which array the English army now hurled itself. The saga says that Hardrada 'fell into such a battle-fury that he rushed ahead of his men, fighting two-handed so that neither helmets nor mail corselets could withstand him, and all those who stood in his path gave way. It looked then as if the English were on the point of breaking in flight … But now King Harald was struck in the throat by an arrow, and that was his death-wound. He fell, as did all those who had advanced with him, except for those who retreated with the king's banner.' Earl Tostig then took command, and when the surviving Norsemen were offered quarter by Harold Godwinsson they called back that they would rather die. This, Tostig and most of the remaining Norsemen did. The saga continues:

> At this point, Eystein Orri arrived from the ships with all the men he had, who were wearing armour. Eystein got King Harald's banner Landwaster and the fighting began for a third time, even more fiercely than before. The English fell in great numbers and were again on the point of breaking in flight. This stage of the battle was called Orri's Storm. Eystein and his men had run all the way from the ships [where they had received news of the battle from mounted messengers despatched by Hardrada], so fast that they were exhausted and almost unable to fight by the time they arrived; but then they fell into such a battle-fury that they did not even bother to protect themselves with their shields as long as they could still stand. At length they even threw off their mail corselets, and after that it was easy for the English to land blows on them; but others fell and died of exhaustion without so much as a wound on them. Nearly all the leading Norwegians were killed there.

> This happened in the late afternoon. As was to be expected, not everyone reacted in the same way; some fled, and others were lucky enough to escape in various ways. Darkness had fallen before the carnage finally came to an end.

The *Anglo-Saxon Chronicle* says that the Norsemen were pursued all the way back to their ships at Riccall, and that there were few survivors. These were allowed to sail for home in just 24 ships, leaving the flower of Norwegian manhood stretched dead behind them.

Although occasional raids on England continued to be recorded until as late as 1151, and Scandinavian pirates from the Orkneys and the Western Isles were still active even later, it is readily apparent why 1066 is generally taken to mark the end of the Viking era, and why Harald Hardrada is often dubbed 'the last Viking'. His was the last great enterprise of the Viking Age. Night was now falling on the long Viking day that had begun nearly 300 years earlier.

The Vikings in North America

From the time that Christopher Columbus made the European discovery of America in 1492, there were rumours that there might have been previous and unrecorded European explorers to the vast new lands out west. As early as the 3rd century BC, there were tales of Phoenicians that had ventured beyond Gibraltar and reached 'Thule', which is now generally believed to be the west coast of Norway rather than the American Arctic. Some raised the possibility that Egyptians or Romans might have reached Central America.

A sounder, if still extremely vague, account is that of the Irish monks led by Saint Brendan, who might have discovered the New World to the west during the 6th century AD. The folklore tale known as the 'Voyage of Saint Brendan' has many intriguing aspects besides its fantastic and mythical aspect. The island with a volcano might well be Iceland; the phenomenon described as a silver column, hard as marble and looking like crystal, may have been the sighting of an iceberg. There can be no doubt that the monks did travel in Arctic seas. Recent experiments with a reconstruction of an ancient Irish boat proved the seaworthiness of such craft in the North Atlantic. It thus seems that explorer monks might have ventured west but no further evidence has been uncovered to prove that they did in fact reach America.

The Viking sagas

Until the 1960s, this was also generally the case with the tales of Viking voyages to the New World. Less than two centuries ago, it was agreed Vikings had reached Iceland and even Greenland during the Middle Ages but little else

VIKING VOYAGES IN THE NORTH ATLANTIC

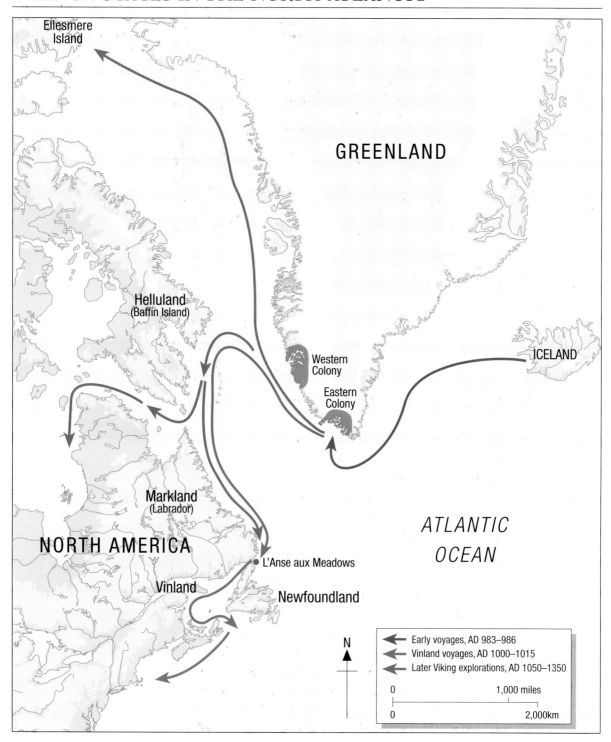

Ellesmere Island

GREENLAND

Helluland
(Baffin Island)

ICELAND

Western
Colony

Eastern
Colony

Markland
(Labrador)

NORTH AMERICA

ATLANTIC
OCEAN

L'Anse aux Meadows

Vinland

Newfoundland

N

Early voyages, AD 983–986
Vinland voyages, AD 1000–1015
Later Viking explorations, AD 1050–1350

0   1,000 miles

0   2,000km

Brattahild, the eastern settlement, founded by Erik the Red. The settlement was founded around AD 1000 and for the next few centuries thrived as a Norse colony. It was finally abandoned due to the deterioration of the climate. (Werner Forman Archive)

was known for certain. The modern debate over the discovery of America by the Vikings started in 1837, when a Danish scholar, Professor Carl Christian Rafn, published his *American Antiquities*. This contained two sagas recounting voyages by Vikings made some eight centuries earlier to a western land that had all the appearances of being America. The *Greenlanders' Saga* and the *Saga of Erik the Red* both related with some detail the accidental discovery and subsequent exploration of a vast land to the west where short-lived settlements had been attempted. Many details were somewhat contradictory as each tale seems to represent, respectively, the Greenlanders' and the Icelanders' version of the events. The matter-of-fact style of these sagas, devoid of monsters and myths, gave them considerable credibility.

Another factor of credibility was that these discoveries would have been made at the time when Vikings were descending on almost every country in Europe that could be reached by their ships. As part of this movement of expansion, the Vikings reached and settled Iceland from about AD 870. In the middle of the 10th century its population had reached about 30,000 souls. Greenland was eventually sighted, but it was not until about 980 that an expedition landed there and that Erik the Red – apparently so-called because he was a redhead – sought settlers to colonize it. In 986, he founded the two settlements known as the Eastern and Western colonies, which soon had about 3,000 Viking inhabitants.

Sighting America

Also in 986, a merchant from Iceland, Bjarni Herjolfsson, was sailing in the area when his ship was blown off course. Bjarni and his men had, says the *Greenlanders' Saga*, sailed three days 'until the land sank below the horizon'. But then 'a north wind and fog set in, and they did not know in which direction they were sailing.' These poor conditions lasted some time; however, 'eventually, the sun appeared and they were able to take their bearings. They then hoisted their sail and sailed on for a whole day, when they sighted land.'

The crew asked if it was Greenland, but Bjarni said he did not think so. Sailing closer, they saw 'that the land had no mountains, was covered with woods and there were low hills'. Bjarni and his men did not go ashore. They sailed on 'for two days and then sighted a new land' which was 'flat and covered with forests'. They then 'turned the prow away from the land and sailed out to sea before a south-westerly wind for three days when they sighted a third land. This land was high and mountainous and there were glaciers there.' They sailed on and eventually saw that it was an island. They did not land there either, as it seemed 'a worthless land' to Bjarni, but sailed on, were caught in a gale and, after four days of sailing, reached Greenland.

This voyage, and the relative ease of the ones to follow, was in great part due to the prevailing winds and currents around Greenland. The currents on both sides of Greenland flow from north to south, going further along the coast of Labrador until they meet below Newfoundland with the warm Gulf Stream currents flowing north. The winds blow from north to south between Iceland and Greenland, round the southern tip of Greenland and up its west coast. However, further out to sea, the north-west winds blow down from the Arctic, meeting, south of Newfoundland, the warmer winds blowing east.

Bjarni's story intrigued the recent settlers of Greenland. At around AD 1000, Leif Eriksson, the son of Erik the Red, 'came to see Bjarni Herjolfsson, purchased his ship and hired a crew; there were 35 men altogether'. They sailed west from Greenland and 'found first the land which Bjarni had seen last. They lowered a boat and went ashore but did not see any grass there. The highlands consisted of huge glaciers and between the glaciers and the shore, the land was just one single slab of rock. The land seemed to be of no value.' Leif called it 'Helluland' (Flat Stone Land).

Sailing south, they 'found the second land' and went ashore there also. 'The country was flat and covered with forests, and wherever they went were white sandy beaches sloping gently down to the sea.' Leif called it 'Markland' (Forest Land). They then sailed on 'before a north-east wind and were at sea for two days before sighting land'. They went ashore and explored the surroundings. They sighted a river which, they found as they sailed up, 'flowed out of a lake'. Leif and his companions unloaded their gear there and built huts. 'They later decided to winter there and built large houses.' This first Viking settlement in the New World was called 'Leifsbudir'. The land itself was 'so bountiful that it seemed to them that the cattle would not need fodder during the winter. There was no frost in winter and the grass hardly withered. Day and night were of more equal length then they were in Greenland and Iceland.' More explorations brought the discovery of 'vines and grapes' which brought this land the name 'Vinland'. In the spring, they loaded up their ship with timber and went back to Greenland. On the way home they rescued the crew of another ship.

Reproductions of Viking personal items at the L'Anse aux Meadows Visitors Centre, including cloak pins and arm-bands. Few artefacts remain from the original settlement. (© Parks Canada/A Cornellier/ H.01.11.06.01.02)

A *strandhögg* on the *Skraelings*

According to the sagas, there were at least four other expeditions to Vinland from Greenland tentatively dated from about AD 1000 to 1030. The first of these was led by Leif's brother, Thorvald, who with 35 men found the houses previously built by Leif's expedition at Leifsbudir. Up to this time, the Vikings had found no sign of other human life in the new countries until an exploring

A strandhögg. When the need arose to replenish a longship's stores the Vikings would indulge in a strandhögg. Overseas, revictualling continued to depend on 'strandhewing', which was also an excuse for rounding up young women and healthy youths for the thriving slave-trade, and for relieving the locals of whatever gold or valuables they had failed to hide in time. (Angus McBride © Osprey Publishing Ltd)

party 'on an island to the west found a grain holder made of wood' which was obviously man-made. The next summer, Thorvald and his companions had a dramatic first encounter with the natives of the New World. Near a beach, they came upon 'three skin boats with three men under each boat'. Thorvald and his men attacked the aborigines and 'captured all of them except one who got away in his skin boat. They killed the eight men.' This, according to the *Greenlanders' Saga*, was the first encounter between Europeans and Native Americans.

The Vikings called them *Skraelings* ('Wretches' or 'Screechers'), a word encompassing all indigenous peoples without distinction. This action seems to have been a manifestation of one of the most frightful of Viking practices, the *strandhögg*, a coastal raid for rounding up cattle and sheep, and for securing young women and youths for the slave-trade. The aborigines did not let this outrage go by without retort and revenge, proof that the *Skraelings* of Vinland were a brave and determined warrior race. Shortly after this bloody incident, numerous natives came in 'a great number of skin boats' to attack the Viking ship. They were armed with bows which they used skilfully, killing Thorvald, the Viking leader, with an arrow that passed between the ship's gunwale and his shield. Despite this confrontation, the Vikings remained another two years at Leifsbudir in Vinland before returning to Greenland.

To what ethnic group belonged these indigenous warriors, who were audacious enough not only to resist the Vikings, but also to attack them with considerable skill and determination? Some indications would suggest that they were Inuits, and others, that they were North American woodland Indians. The *Saga of Erik the Red* describes them as 'small [or dark] ugly men with coarse hair; they had big eyes and broad cheekbones'. They dressed with animal hides and carried weapons. Were these natives inhabiting Vinland around the year 1000 the ancestors of the Beothuks and Algonquins of the historical period? The question remains essentially unanswered even today, although what evidence there is seems to lean towards woodland Indians.

Evidence

The sagas relating these and other stirring events raised enormous popular interest on both sides of the Atlantic, as a great deal of what they claimed was verifiable and fitted in with the early history of the Vikings' navigation in the North Atlantic. From 1837 and for well over a century, there were innumerable theories peppered with tenuous evidence written as 'proof' of the Vikings' presence in North America. Some calculations made from the sagas' remarks about daylight hours in Vinland being more even throughout the year than Scandinavia put the Vikings as far south as present-day Florida.

Ruins, thought to be from the Viking constructions, made one enthusiastic 19th-century researcher imagine a whole Viking city beneath downtown Boston. An old stone tower in Newport, Rhode Island, with an unusual style of architecture was attributed to the Vikings, when it was in fact a large windmill built in the 17th century. A stone with ancient Norse inscriptions 'discovered' at the end of the 19th century at Kensington, Minnesota, along with others later 'found' in Maine and even as far as Paraguay all turned out to be fraudulent fakes. An interesting twist to fake discoveries occurred in 1936 when a prospector claimed to have found Viking weapons in the wilderness near Beardmore, in north-western Ontario. The rusty swords were indeed authentic Viking weapons, but it was later found that they had been brought to Canada from Norway in the 20th century.

More serious evidence was the so-called Vinland map, made around 1440, discovered in 1957, made public in 1965, discredited as a fake in 1974 and reinstated as authentic in 1986, following much more gruelling tests thanks to scientific advances. The reason for all this excitement was that this world map shows the location of Vinland as west of Greenland. Another map by Segurdur Stefansson found in the Danish Royal Library and dating from the end of the 16th century – after Columbus' discovery of America – nevertheless still shows Helluland, Markland, Skalingeland and a narrow peninsula said to be the 'Promontorium Winlandia', which looks strangely like the long north-west peninsula of Newfoundland.

Discovery of a Viking settlement in Newfoundland

However, there was no conclusive material proof of the Vikings actually reaching and making settlements in America until Norwegian writer Helge Ingstad and his wife Anne Steene correctly surmised that a part of Vinland must be the tip of Newfoundland's peninsula. In 1960, they discovered the remains of a Viking settlement near the little village of L'Anse aux Meadows situated near Épaves Bay in Newfoundland. In subsequent archaeological excavations by Ingstad, Steene and also Bengt Schonback and Brigitta Wallace, the foundations of seven houses were found, one of these being 20 metres (66 feet) long with several rooms and a corridor. The archaeological findings made over the next few years proved without a doubt that around the year 1000 there was a small Viking settlement there. Traces of fireplaces were found, and among the artefacts brought out was a brass pin of the sort used by Vikings to fasten a cape. Another fascinating bit of evidence was a small spinning whorl such as those used by Viking women, a sure indication of their presence there along with the men. The foundations of the houses indicated a style of sod-covered house very much like those in Greenland and Iceland.

These extraordinary discoveries proved conclusively that the Vikings had indeed been to America five centuries before Columbus. L'Anse aux Meadows became a Canadian National Historic Site and a UNESCO World Heritage Site. Thus, long dismissed by some to be simply legendary stories with grains of truth, the tales of exploration that make up the *Greenlanders' Saga* and the *Saga of Erik the Red* were now confirmed. It would indeed seem that Newfoundland was the 'Vinland' of the sagas.

The discovery also prompted many new questions as to the Vikings in America and what they reportedly saw as related in the sagas. If this was Vinland, where were the grapes, the lush vegetation reported by the tales of the Greenlanders and of Erik the Red? Part of the answer probably lies in that the climate in the area was milder around AD 1000. Until the end of the 13th century, the climate of the northern hemisphere was somewhat warmer but thereafter became progressively colder until the middle of the 19th century when it again became warmer. During this period know as the 'Little Ice Age' people could skate on the Thames and on canals in Holland, while crops failed in northern Europe and northern China. On the whole, the more temperate countries coped reasonably well with this colder climate. In the more northerly parts of the hemisphere, however, the results were far more severe. Whatever grew in Greenland and areas further west would now have much more difficulty surviving. An increase in icebergs chased the whales further south so that the food supply of Inuits in the far north was much affected, prompting many to migrate. Thus, more vegetation would have grown in Vinland around AD 1000. It has also been suggested, quite sensibly, that Leif Eriksson gave it an attractive name to draw settlers just as his father had done with Greenland.

Whatever the present vegetation, the Vikings settled there in a past that was more lush. But how long did they remain? What did they do there? Was

this the only settlement, and why did they abandon it? Did they explore elsewhere? For some of the answers, one must again go back to the sagas. They are the nearest thing we have to a history of the Vikings in North America, and their tales are full of drama.

Settling in Vinland

After the return of Thorvald's expedition sometime after AD 1000, a couple of years passed until another Viking visit was made to Vinland. This time, the stated aim was to establish a sizeable settlement in Vinland. This colonizing expedition was organized in Greenland. It was made up of 60 men and five women with some livestock and was under a leader named Thorfinn Karlsefni. They sailed and arrived safely at Leifsbudir in Vinland, and the account mentions that they had plenty of food 'with all kinds of game and fish and other things' and busied themselves gathering timber, a scarce commodity in Greenland. Also at about this time, Gutrid, the wife of Karlsefni, gave birth in the Vinland settlement to a boy named Snorri, the first known child of European parents born in America. Furthermore, according to the *Greenlanders' Saga*, Karlsefni 'had a formidable stockade built round his houses and they [his men] made preparations to defend themselves'. This was the first reported fortification of some importance built by Europeans in America.

The sagas report that Viking colonists in Vinland carried swords, axes and spears. They do not mention any archers in their ranks. The main items of defensive equipment were shields. They had red shields for battle and a white

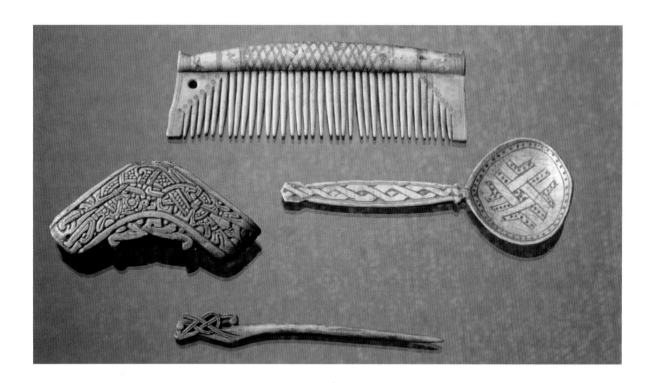

shield that was used as a sign of peace. Coats of mail were seldom worn by Vikings because of their high cost. Probably only leaders and the wealthiest individuals had them. However, we do know that coats of mail came to America, as witnessed by two fragments dating respectively from the 11th and 12th centuries that were discovered during archaeological excavations in north-western Greenland and eastern Ellesmere Island.

The Viking colonists spent the winter in the Vinland settlement. They saw no traces of the *Skraelings* until the next summer when 'great numbers of them emerged from the woods' nearby. The natives were reportedly terrified by the bellowing of the cattle brought by the Vikings, which caused some confusion especially as 'neither party could understand the other's language'. As a 'token of peace' the Vikings decided to 'take a white shield and carry it towards them'. This worked. Eventually it was understood that the *Skraelings* wanted to trade with the Vikings.

According to the *Saga of Erik the Red*, Karlsefni and his men 'raised their shields', and the natives and the Vikings 'began to trade'. What first most attracted the *Skraelings* 'was red cloth', which they 'tied round their heads'. They would offer fur pelts, as they had 'grey furs and sables and skins of all kinds' to exchange. They also wanted to purchase swords and spears, but both sagas relate that Karlsefni strictly 'forbade his men to sell them weapons'. Trading between

More reproductions of Viking artefacts from the Visitors Centre at L'Anse aux Meadows. A number of Viking-era combs have been found, pointing to the value their culture placed on good grooming. (© Parks Canada / A Cornellier / H.01.11.06.01.01)

the *Skraelings* and the Vikings 'continued like this for some time' until the Vikings ran out of cloth. A bull happened to run out of the forest 'bellowing loudly', which greatly scared the natives who 'ran for their boats and rowed south along the shore. After that, they did not see the natives for three weeks.'

Fighting the *Skraelings*

These relatively friendly relations turned sour when some natives returned, and according to the *Greenlanders' Saga*, one was killed by the Vikings for trying to 'steal' weapons. Whatever happened, the *Saga of Erik the Red* now reported 'a multitude of native boats approaching from the south' with natives armed with staves 'and all … were howling loudly'. The Vikings 'raised their red shields which they carried against them' and they 'clashed and fought fiercely. There was a hail of missiles and the natives used war slings also.' The *Skraelings* were 'putting up on poles a large blue-black ball-shaped object. This they sent flying through the air towards Karlsefni's men and it made a hideous sound when it came down. This so frightened Karlsefni and his men that their only thought was to flee along the river to some steep cliffs and there they made a stand.' At this point, Freydis, the sister of the previously slain Thorvald, came out of a house and saw the Vikings fleeing. She shouted, 'Why run away from these wretches? Such brave men as you are … If I only had a sword, I would fight better than any of you!' But they did not listen, and Freydis, although she was 'slow on her feet since she was with child,' managed to join them in the forest 'pursued by the natives'. There she saw a dead Viking 'with a flat stone buried in his head,' and she picked up his sword 'in order to defend herself with it' as the *Skraelings* came rushing towards her. 'Then she pulled out her breasts from under her shift and slapped them with the sword. The natives were so terrified that they ran off to their boats and rowed away. Karlsefni and his men came over and praised her for her courage.'

In this engagement with its rather bizarre conclusion, the Vikings had two men killed in exchange for the slaying of four, or 'many' (depending on which source is believed), of the natives. It had been a close call for the Viking settlement. The colonists started wondering what would happen if they were attacked simultaneously by natives in boats and on the land side. The *Skraelings* came well armed with slings as well as bows and arrows. Projectiles had 'rained down like hail' on the Vikings. There was also the natives' curious spherical object, which had terrified Karlsefni and his men.

The *Skraelings* as warriors

According to the first European explorers, all the various peoples scattered across America had warlike traditions. Although very brief, these tales from the sagas corroborate several pieces of information about the military arts of the *Skraelings*. They were, apparently, quite well organized in a military sense. The sagas tell us that, in effect, they could mobilize very large numbers of warriors in a short time and move them to the threatened area to engage in battle. Courage in battle was valued in their culture, for they were prepared to attack an unknown and fearsome-looking people on ships or inside a settlement, as is recorded in the sagas. They were also very mobile, due in large part to the lightness of their skin boats, and capable of rapid retreat, which was not necessarily the defeat and rout that the Vikings thought. They would retreat, regroup, be reinforced and attack even more fiercely. As the later Europeans in America were to learn over centuries of battles with the natives, lightning attacks followed by quick withdrawals were typical of their method of waging war.

Finally, the natives obviously handled their Stone-Age weapons extremely well as proven by the Viking killed by a 'flat stone buried in his head'. We must recall here that they only had weapons of wood, bone, sharp rocks and sinews against men armed with steel swords and steel-tipped spears. The *Skraelings* also had a knowledge of the psychology of combat, having invented objects intended to terrify the enemy, like the blue-black balls thrown at the Vikings. So far as reconnaissance was concerned, the Vikings, though unfamiliar with the country, do not appear to have been very good scouts. They do not seem to have discovered the location of the natives' bases or villages in order to attack them on the spot, while the natives certainly located and attacked the European settlements very quickly. This reveals the existence of an effective surveillance system, which must have been in place to protect their own villages from other hostile natives. One may also wonder at the sort of commotion the arrival of the Vikings must have had on the natives and their society. Were the numerous *Skraelings* attacking the Vikings from one nation? Or were they a larger gathering of many native nations to counter what was perceived as an extraordinary threat? The utter violence of the Vikings on the natives as well as among themselves had nothing to recommend them and may well have mobilized the natives to drive them out. In any event, the counterattacks of the *Skraelings* finally sealed the fate of any further attempts at setting up colonies in Vinland. As the *Saga of Erik the Red* says, the Vikings 'realized that even though this was good land, their lives here would always be dominated by battle and fear' – quite a statement for a Viking to make.

The reasons for abandoning the Vinland settlement were most likely a combination of increasing internal strife between various Viking leaders as illustrated by the wholesale murder of the colony ordered by Freydis recounted in the *Greenlanders' Saga*, and the increasing pressure of the *Skraelings*

A battle between Vikings and Skraelings, 11th century. The principal reason for the failure of the Vikings' attempts at permanent settlement in North America was clearly their hostile relationship with the Skraelings, as the sagas call the Indians and Eskimos alike. Anthropologists have tentatively identified them with the extinct Micmac or Beothuk Indians, related to the Algonquins. The Skraelings responsible for the eventual extinction of the Greenland settlements were Eskimos rather than Indians. (Angus McBride © Osprey Publishing Ltd)

who also had axes to grind regarding the treatment that they had received from the violent and strange newcomers.

Later Viking explorations

The events related in the sagas happened in the first years after AD 1000. Thereafter, the sagas remain silent on further voyages or settlements to the west of Greenland. Although evidence is still scant, there can be no doubt that there were further voyages from Greenland in the centuries to follow. One of the most important discoveries in that regard was made in 1978 by archaeologist Peter Schledermann at Ellesmere Island in the Canadian Arctic. Here, a piece of medieval chain mail was found. This was followed by iron boat rivets, pieces of knives and a scale. Some Inuit wood statuettes, crude as they were, obviously showed figures in European dress. One particularly striking example found by archaeologist Deborah Sabo on Baffin Island

Carving of a European (replica) from Baffin Island, Eastern Arctic, c. 1300. This tiny wooden figure was excavated in 1977 from a Thule Inuit site on southern Baffin Island. It is carved in typical Thule Inuit style, but depicts an individual wearing a long robe with split front and edge trim that resembles European dress of the time. A faintly incised cross is carved on the chest. (© Canadian Museum of Civilization, no. KeDq-7:325, photo Harry Foster, no. S94-6299)

represents a man in a long and ample tunic trimmed with a border in front and around the skirt with what appears to be a cross hanging on the chest. None of these features can be related to Inuit costume, so it is obviously meant to represent a medieval European. All these objects dated from the 12th and 13th centuries. While found in Inuit sites on the island, they obviously came with traders from Greenland who had sailed as far as Ellesmere Island. From this, we can gather that the Vikings came well armed with protective clothing including chain mail as well as tools to weigh and measure what was being traded.

Another aspect of Viking explorations of the North Atlantic was that the Viking colonies in Iceland and Greenland, pagan at the time of the Vinland explorations, were converted to Christianity shortly thereafter. Thus the sign of the cross arrived as a symbol that would have been worn by these early Nordic Christians, which explains the cross on the statuette. Christianity also brought a new and more charitable view of life and a respect for the lives and property of others. Certainly, it would appear that the following centuries of exploration and trade by the Vikings into lands to the west were less violent and barbaric than the desperate fighting with *Skraelings*. A number of sites in the eastern Canadian Arctic featuring ancient foundations made of stone have been claimed to be Viking dwellings made between the 11th and the 13th centuries but conclusive proof, such as found at L'Anse aux Meadows, has not been found as yet. Stones were also used by ancient aborigines in the area. If they did not have permanent settlements, the Vikings certainly traded with the Inuits who migrated eastward across the Arctic and on to Greenland from about the 11th century.

The two Viking colonies in Greenland never grew to be large communities. As time passed, they became more and more isolated from Norway and Denmark, which simply forgot their existence. There were increasing contacts between the Greenland Viking settlers and the Inuits, some of them violent according to later sagas. By about 1350, the western settlement had been abandoned and a tale related that, in 1418, the eastern settlement had been attacked with many churches set ablaze by *Skraelings*. Until recently, the common interpretation had been that the settlements had perished under *Skraeling* attacks but this is now challenged. Archaeological findings reveal a much more complex pattern, as they show considerable contacts and trade between Vikings and Inuits for at least two centuries. There surely were occasional armed disputes, but the most likely reason for the failure of the Greenland colonies is now thought to be the economic abandonment by northern Europe of these far-away settlements. No more ships were sent to Greenland. With few items left to trade and probably suffering the first effects of the Little Ice Age, the Vikings had left Greenland by the middle of the 15th century, a land that was now totally forgotten by continental Europe.

The Viking Hersir

A CULTURE OF VIOLENCE

When Norwegian Vikings first raided the European coast in the 8th century AD, their leaders were not kings, princes or *jarls*, but a middle rank of warrior known as the *hersir*. At this time the *hersir* was typically an independent landowner or local chieftain. His equipment was usually superior to that of his followers. By the end of the 10th century, the independence of the *hersir* was gone, and he was now typically a regional servant of the Norwegian king. The *hersir's* equipment and status were now comparable to that of an immediate retainer of the Scandinavian or English king, similar, for example, to a Huscarl at the time of the battle of Hastings.

As mentioned in 'A History of the Vikings', the earliest violent appearance of Norwegians on the coast of Britain is recorded in the *Anglo-Saxon Chronicle* for the year 789. Whether or not one views the murder of King Beorhtric's reeve as an act of raiding, the chronicler confidently asserts, 'These were the first ships of the Danes to come to England.' In reality, they appear to have been Norwegians from the district of Hjordaland.

The fact that the earliest sources are written from the perspective of the Anglo-Saxon Church may well have distorted our knowledge of the earliest phases of Viking raiding in England. We know that Offa was preparing the defences of Kent against pagan seamen as early as 792, and although our source is not specific we may suspect that these were Scandinavian pirates. The terms pagans, pirates and seamen had become synonymous with the Vikings by the end of the period. The apparent concentration of early raids on the monasteries of Lindisfarne (793) and Iona (795) probably conceals a picture of more widespread depredations. Continental raids show no such bias against the religious. The raiders off the Loire in 799, for example, are not noted as seeking out monastic communities. The Danish assault in 810 on the Carolingian province of Frisia and the subsequent attack in 820 may have been directed against important trading centres. Certainly by the mid-830s settlements of economic importance had become the main targets of Viking attentions.

A Viking horseman, with full armour, on a 12th-century tapestry from Baldishol Church, Norway. Note the kite-shaped shield and helmet with noseguard. By this time Viking equipment and dress had evolved significantly under western influence. (CM Dixon/The Ancient Art & Architecture Collection Ltd)

The emphasis in Old English records on the ecclesiastical bias of Nordic raids is one aspect of the cultural divide between Scandinavians and Christian Europeans in the 8th century. Even in Denmark, the most advanced of the three Scandinavian 'nations', the relationship of basic units of society to the elite class was very different to that in north-western Europe. The absence of a unified church or even a common religion weakened the possibility of a single national monarchy appearing.

The lack of a central authority meant that the use of violence by the individual, tribe or clan was institutionalized and accepted as inevitable. The increasingly powerful monarchies of the various English kingdoms were able to prevent violence by legislation that carried the sanction of the church. This intimate relationship of church and state limited aggression in a way Viking culture could not. Consequently, when circumstance allowed Scandinavian intrusions into broadly peaceful continental Europe, the unlimited use of violence (a feature of everyday life in the Nordic lands) found lucrative outlets.

TRAINING

In early Scandinavian society, the normal unit of warfare was the tribe. The sub-divisions of this were the family or clan. The Old Norse word for these extended family groups was *aett*. In the *Elder Edda*, this is used to describe

Angantyr and his sons, effectively a military unit (said to be berserkers) laid in a mass grave after their defeat and death. In a culture where the family was the fundamental combat group, training would, largely speaking, be part of everyday life.

Non blood-related loyalties were largely based around what is perhaps best termed the 'Gift Economy', which centred around the relationship between leader and followers. This relationship could often become elevated to a level more normal to bonds of kinship. In effect, it resulted in the formation of 'Artificial Clans'. Other versions of these simulated clans may have existed in groups of alienated, landless young men who gathered on the fringes of society and made a living by banditry and warfare. Such elements may have been the basis for the Norse stories of berserkers. In some sagas berserkers appear in groups of vagabond outlaws. In the society of early medieval Iceland, where so much depended on the family, landholding and well-defined rights of settlement, berserkers are seen as rootless outsiders (see page 102).

Several forms of the oath that legitimized the 'Artificial Clan' survive in the sagas. One appears in *Gisli's Saga*, where it is described in the following terms:

A long sod is cut from the turf, with both ends still attached to the ground; this is held up by a spear with a pattern-welded blade, the shaft of which is so long that a man with an outstretched arm can just reach the rivets that hold the head in position. Those who are making the bond mingle their blood into the earth scratched up under the sod; kneeling they then swear an oath and shake hands, calling the gods to witness that they will avenge one another.

Another artificial extension of the family group was the system of fostering. Young children or adolescents could be sent to live in a separate household. Such arrangements did not normally exceed the boundaries of the clan, the most common form of fostering being to an uncle. Early Germanic languages have several words describing the very particular relationships that

Detail of a spear socket with inlaid 'herringbone' pattern in silver. Several similar Norwegian examples are at the National Museum, Oslo. (© Copyright the Trustees of the British Museum, MME 1893, 0715.2)

85

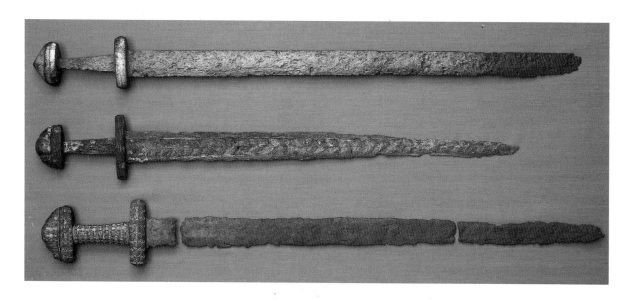

Decorated Danish sword hilts. The large pommel served as a counterweight to the blade, making the sword easier to handle in the strenuous style of swordplay that prevailed in the Viking Age. We are told that swordsmen 'did not strike fast and furiously, but took their time and picked their strokes carefully, so that they were few but terrible. More regard was given to the weight of each blow than to the number struck.' (The National Museum of Denmark)

were established by this system. In the household of their foster-parent, the duties of a young male would be identical to those of a son by birth – including training for war.

In the earliest phase of the Viking Age all training would depend on these various forms of clan or pseudo-clan. Older members of the *aett* would pass on their knowledge of fighting techniques to the younger clan members, either in formal training sessions or possibly by passing on oral traditions. The latter might take the form of stories of past deeds or the lives of past heroes, stressing the obligations of a warrior.

The particular brand of explosive violence that was the hallmark of Egil Skallagrimson was encouraged at an early stage by Thord Granison. Thord is described in *Egil's Saga* as young but older than Egil. Egil persuaded Thord to take him to the annual winter sports at White-river-dale in Iceland. When Egil fell into an argument with Grim Heggson which led to blows, it was Thord who equipped and supported Egil for the slaying of Grim. At this time Egil was less than 12 years old. A similar incident occurs in the early life of Grettir Asmundson, although this does not end with a death, only threats of revenge. Grettir's first man-killing takes place when he is about 15 years old. If any reliance can be placed on these accounts, a picture of society emerges dominated by violence as an everyday means of settling minor disputes. Adolescent males are not excluded from this aspect of life, and extreme behaviour was modified by relatively mild correction. By these means, the required attitude for a life of warfare was developed in the young. The semi-martial nature of the games that led Egil and Grettir to violence would

give exercise and training in the handling of real weapons. The massive concentration in Old Norse sources on weapon-handling skills, recounted for the amazement and admiration of the reader, offers us an insight into the importance of such abilities to the Viking warrior.

The Jomsvikings

As the independence of the minor states in Norway was eroded, several options were left to those who did not wish to submit to the dynasty of Harald Harfagri. The first of these was settlement in another part of Europe, where the rulers were less powerful or capable of being overthrown (for example in the Saxon kingdoms or the 'Norman' areas of Neustria). For the established

A mail corselet from Verdal, Nord-Trøndelag, Norway. Archaeological and saga evidence indicates that those worn in the 8th–11th centuries were identical. (© Museum of Cultural History, University of Oslo, Norway, photographer Louis Smestad)

middle-ranking landowners with a certain amount of movable wealth and ambition, colonization of unpopulated Iceland was preferred. For the landless warrior, the old form of raiding in loose bands was losing its viability. The defences of western Europe were able to turn back all but the largest hosts. These extended raiding bands were held together by allegiance to important figures like Rolf the Gänger. The formation of the *Jomsvikingelag*, or Jomsvikings, an artificial tribe, was a reaction to this stiffening of resistance. New levels of organization and training were achieved which allowed a penetration of the English kingdoms by this large war-band.

According to later Danish accounts, the Jomsvikings were established in Wendland in the late 10th century (probably the 980s) by King Harald Bluetooth of Denmark, banished from his own kingdom by his son Swein Forkbeard. The fortress of Jomsborg, which he reputedly founded, was probably at or near Wollin, Adam of Bremen's Jumne, at the mouth of the Oder. It had an artificial harbour, its entrance guarded by a tower over a stone archway with iron gates, reported in the oldest extant manuscript as being capable of holding three ships – a figure later increased to 300 or 360. One version says that Harald taught the Wends piracy, and Jomsborg itself may in fact have been garrisoned by Wends commanded by Danes; certainly at the battle of Svöldr one of the 11 Jomsviking ships present was crewed by Wends. The *Jomsvikings' Saga*, however, would have it that Jomsborg was a purely Viking stronghold established by Swein

Two typical Viking swords frame two period spearheads. (© Copyright the Trustees of the British Museum)

Forkbeard's foster-father, Pálnatóki. Either way, most accounts seem to agree that the leader of the Jomsvikings in their heyday at the end of the 10th century was Earl Sigvald, son of a petty king named Strut-Harald, who had ruled over Scania in Sweden (at this time counted as part of Denmark).

Icelandic records give a list of the laws that underpinned the Jomsvikings' military society. The *Jomsvikings' Saga* records these as follows:

1. No man older than 50 or younger than 18 to be enrolled.
2. Kinship not to be taken into consideration on enrolment.
3. No man to run from an inferior opponent.
4. Jomsvikings to avenge one another as brothers.
5. No man to indicate fear by speech regardless of events.
6. Plunder to be held in common on pain of expulsion.
7. No one to stir up contention.
8. No spreading of rumours. The leader to disseminate all news.
9. No man to have a woman within the fortress.
10. No one to be absent more than three days.
11. The leader to have the final say in any dispute over kin-slaying which may have occurred outside the Jomsviking brotherhood.

Caution is required when attempting to treat the above as an exact account of the rules under which this early medieval unit operated. The laws are intended to supersede outside loyalties and replace them with new duties and obedience to the Jomsviking. Some parallels to individual laws can be found in *Half's Saga ok Halfsrekka* and echo some of the customs of the *hird* as found in the *Hirdskra*. Jomsviking training went beyond weapon skills. The greatest innovation of this code was the application of older schemes and frameworks of loyalty to new conditions.

Although relatives were often recruited contrary to the laws, a form of selection appears to have been practised. Half of the followers of Sigvaldi Strut-Haraldson were turned away when their leader joined the organization. In its use of selective recruitment, the replacement of societal ties by new obligations to an artificial body and the imposition of a governing code, the Jomsviking brotherhood has many similarities to more modern methods of organizing military formations.

'Every summer they went out and made war in different countries, got high renown, and were looked on as the greatest of warriors; hardly any others were thought their equals at this time.' So says the *Jomsvikings' Saga*, while *King Olaf Tryggvasson's Saga* observes that 'at that time it was considered prestigious to have

Viking warriors on a raid. Their dress is typical of the 9th–10th centuries, though the mail corselet worn by the centre figure was more common in the 11th century. Note the bow and arrow carried by the figure on the right. (Angus McBride © Osprey Publishing Ltd)

Jomsborg Vikings with an army'. The truth of the matter would appear to be somewhat different, however, since all three of the major campaigns in which the sources claim the brotherhood participated ended in disaster for their employers: Styrbjorn Starki, contending for the throne of Sweden, was beaten by his uncle, Erik the Victorious, at Fyrisvold near Uppsala; Swein Forkbeard's attack on Earl Hakon of Norway was disastrously defeated at Hjdrungavag *c.* 990; and King Olaf Tryggvasson of Norway was defeated and killed by the Swedes and Danes at Svöldr in 1000. All three defeats appear to have resulted from the same cause – that Earl Sigvald had a nasty tendency to cut and run if the prospects began to look dubious! This is probably why *King Olaf Tryggvasson's Saga* describes him as 'a prudent, ready-minded man'.

King Magnus the Good of Norway destroyed Jomsborg in 1043, 'killing many people, burning and destroying both in the town and in the country

Norwegian decorated spear sockets. The 'winged' one on the right is probably a Frankish import, though the inlay has undoubtedly been added by a Viking craftsman. (© Museum of Cultural History, University of Oslo, Norway, photographer Louis Smestad)

all around, and wreaking the greatest havoc'. However, the nucleus of the Jomsvikings' guild appears to have disbanded much earlier, probably after Earl Sigvald's death some time before 1010. Remnants of the Jomsvikings are said to have accompanied Earl Sigvald's brothers Herring and Thorkell the Tall to England in 1009, where in time they may have become the nucleus of King Cnut's *Tinglith*, the royal bodyguard that was to evolve into the celebrated Huscarls.

Individual weapon skill

The sagas recount numerous tales of individual weapon skill and daring. These deeds give an insight into the abilities that allowed the Norsemen to cut a swathe from the Caspian Sea to North America.

In a wintertime fight, Skarphedin Njalson is reputed to have slid across an ice-sheet, cutting down one man as he went and jumping over a shield thrown to trip him by a second. Olaf Tryggvasson is said to have thrown two javelins at once with ambidextrous skill. On several occasions spears are caught in midflight and returned. The level of ability needed to carry out these exploits would need to be created and maintained by constant practice.

Archery practice, while not institutionalized as a legal requirement as in medieval England, is frequently implied. Einar Tambarskelf was able to shoot a headless arrow through a hide. This trick would be a training exercise requiring concentration, strength and accuracy. Hunting with bows would similarly hone the skills required in warfare.

The hunt encouraged quick thinking and reflexes and was an integral part of the way of life of the warrior class. It was a pastime, a means of destroying destructive pests and of providing food, as illustrated in *Grettir's Saga*, where the hero encounters a troublesome bear.

TACTICS

At sea

The greatest strategic advantage held by the Vikings was their mobility, their freedom to operate within foreign territories. Not bound by treaty or convention, the early raiding bands were able to give rein to the plundering instincts and use the violent tendencies that characterized Scandinavian culture at this time to achieve disruptive results out of proportion to their numbers. As the character of the Viking warrior changed and large-scale, semi-professional armies emerged, it became important to safeguard the gains already made. As a consequence we find the Viking host of 876 swearing peace with Alfred on a sacred ring (which no one had succeeded in forcing them to do before) prior to the settlement of Northumbria.

Viking freedom of action throughout the period was based on the superiority of Scandinavian maritime ability. Alcuin expresses surprise that they were able to descend on the Northumbrian coast in 793. His shock probably owes more to the audacity of the pagans in attacking the monastery of Lindisfarne than to any unexpected improvement in shipbuilding. More important than any superior shipbuilding technique was the skill of the Vikings as sailors. By a combination of sailing instructions passed down from generation to generation, advanced methods of navigation and excellent maritime skills, the Vikings were able to menace any part of Europe with enough water to float their shallow keels.

When fighting amongst themselves, the Vikings' major battles almost invariably took place at sea. All naval engagements were fought close to land, and in some instances the course of battle was affected by coastal features. In 896 three Viking ships were trapped by faulty mooring and destroyed by King Alfred's navy on the Hampshire coast. Suitably trained and equipped defenders were quite capable of matching the Vikings in their own element.

Nevertheless, they made every effort to ensure that a naval action was as much like a land battle as possible, arranging their fleets in lines or wedges; one side – or sometimes both – customarily roped together the largest of their ships gunwale to gunwale to form large, floating platforms. The biggest and best-manned ships usually formed the middle part of the line, with the commander's vessel invariably positioned in the very centre, since he normally had the largest vessel of all. High-sided merchantmen were sometimes positioned on the flanks of the line too. The prows of the longer ships extended out in front of the battle-line and some of them, called *bardi*, were therefore armoured with iron plates at stem and stern, which bore the brunt of the fighting. Some even had a series of iron spikes called a beard (*skegg*) round the prow, designed to hole enemy ships venturing close enough to board.

In addition to this floating platform, there were usually a number of additional individual ships positioned on the flanks and in the rear, whose tasks were to skirmish with their opposite numbers; to attack the enemy platform if he had one; to put reinforcements aboard their own platform when necessary; and to pursue the enemy in flight. Masts were lowered in battle, and all movement was by oar, so the loss of a ship's oars in collision with another vessel effectively crippled it. Nevertheless, the classical *diekplus* manoeuvre, which involved shearing off an enemy vessel's oars with the prow of one's own ship, does not seem to have been deliberately employed, and nor was ramming. The main naval tactic was simply to row against an enemy ship, grapple and board it, and clear it with hand weapons before moving on to another vessel, sometimes cutting the cleared ship loose if it formed the wing of a platform. The platforms were attacked by as many ships as could pull alongside. Boarding was usually preceded by a shower of arrows and, at closer range, javelins, iron-shod stakes and stones, as a result of which each oarsman was often protected by a second man, who deflected missiles with his shield. On the final approach prior to boarding, shields were held overhead 'so closely, that no part of their holders was left uncovered'. Some ships carried extra supplies of stones and other missiles. Stones are extensively recorded in accounts of Viking naval battles, and were clearly the favourite form of missile. The largest were dropped from high-sided vessels on to (and even through) the decks of ships that drew alongside to board.

When raiding, the Vikings preferred to beach their ships on a small island or eyot, or in the curve of a river, throwing up a rampart and stockade on any side that could be approached by land. The resultant fortified encampment was usually left with a garrison, since the Vikings took care to protect their lines of communication: failure to do so could result in utter rout and heavy losses. These camps might also be used as a refuge in face of a superior enemy force: they were rarely attacked successfully, the besiegers tending to disperse after a period of inactivity.

Land-battle formations

In land battles, the Vikings' favoured battle formation was a shield wall, or *skjaldborg* – a massive phalanx of men several ranks deep (apparently five or more) with the better-armed and armoured men forming the front ranks. On occasion they might form up in two or even more such shield walls, as they did at the battles of Ashdown and Meretun in 871, and at Corbridge in 918 (where one of the four divisions they formed was held in reserve in a concealed position). Several units could be deployed in mutually supporting *skjaldborgr*, which might also be positioned to mount surprise attacks.

There is some debate as to just how close-packed the shield wall formation actually was. Contemporary literary references indicate that hand-to-hand

A sea battle, based on *King Olaf Tryggvasson's Saga*. This scene depicts the saga's account of the battle of Svöldr. Olaf's ship, the giant *Long Serpent*, is surrounded by those of his enemies, including Earl Eric Hakonsson of Lade in the *Iron Beard*. In the battle's final moments, 'most of the *Serpent*'s men had been killed, brave and stout though they were. Finally King Olaf and Kolbjorn the marshal both leapt overboard, one on each side. But the earl's men had set out their ship's boats all round the *Serpent* and were killing those who leaped overboard. These men tried to seize the king in order to take him to Earl Eric, but King Olaf threw his shield above his head and sank beneath the surface.' (Angus McBride © Osprey Publishing Ltd)

combat involved a considerable degree of violent movement, and the amount of twisting, dodging and leaping back and forth that this entailed makes it seem improbable that the men's shields overlapped. Nevertheless, a 10th-century hogback tombstone in Gosforth, Cumbria, carries a relief of a shield wall in which the shields are overlapped up to about half their width (which would give a frontage of only about 18in [46cm] per man), and the 9th-century Oseberg tapestry similarly includes a shield wall of partially overlapping shields.

Snorri Sturlusson too, in his description of the battle of Stamford Bridge in *King Harald's Saga*, tells us that the Norsemen there drew up with their shields 'overlapping in front and above'. The shield wall was used defensively by Harald Hardrada at Stamford Bridge when he arranged his forces in a circular formation that lacked depth. The rear ranks of this formation locked shields in the same manner as the front rank. Hardrada's advice to his spearmen reflects what was probably standard practice for infantry formations facing a mounted charge (evidence for English cavalry at Stamford Bridge is inconclusive). The front rankers were told to set the butt of their spear to the ground and aim the point at the rider's chest; those in the second line were instructed to level their spear point at the horse. In addition, the bodyguards of Tostig and Harald formed a mobile reserve intended to counter the more dangerous English assaults. This elite unit is said to have included archers who were commanded to give close support to the hand-to-hand fighters.

Scene from the Bayeux Tapestry showing the shield wall at Hastings, formed of heavily equipped men using kite-shaped shields. A single archer — just visible on the far right — provides missile support. (R Sheridan / The Ancient Art & Architecture Collection Ltd)

Viking horseman carved into an 8th-century picture stone at Lillbjärs, Gotland. Note his conical helmet with earguards. The figure beneath the horse's front legs appears to be wearing either mail or a quilted corselet. (Werner Forman Archive/Statens Historiska Museet, Stockholm)

Interestingly, members of a present-day re-enactment organization, the Norse Film and Pageant Society, who use reproductions of Viking weapons and armour, have made the observation that in close combat any extra elbow-room required for a good swing with an axe or sword was best found by pushing into the enemy formation rather than by standing in line in one's own ranks. This would tend to support the hypothesis that shields were probably initially interlocked to receive the impact of the first enemy charge, but that thereafter the shield wall tended to loosen up automatically.

The Vikings' main variation on the simple phalanx was the *svinfylka* or 'swine array', a wedge-shaped formation said to have been invented by Odin himself, a testament to its antiquity. It is more likely to have derived from the 4th- or 5th-century late Roman legionary formation, the *porcinum capet* ('swine head') rather than the teachings of a battle god. Described in *Flateyjarbok* as having two men in the first rank, three in the second and five in the third, it

could be fielded either singly or in multiples joined at the base, the whole line thus resembling a zig-zag.

The Vikings were usually uncomfortable fighting against cavalry, though generally they seem to have succeeded in retiring in good order, and were even capable of rallying and winning the day. The battle of Saucourt in 881, where they are recorded to have lost as many as 8,000–9,000 men, was their first decisive defeat at the hands of Frankish cavalry (who were the best in western Europe at that date), and even that was a close-run thing. When their first attack had seemed successful, the Franks had made the tactical error of breaking ranks in order to start looting, upon which a Viking counterattack nearly broke them. A second charge by the Franks forced the Vikings to withdraw, once again in good order despite their incredibly heavy losses. In the East, too, they are recorded as being at a disadvantage when confronted by cavalry, as in the fighting with the Byzantines around Silistria in 972. A rare instance of Vikings facing feudal cavalry is recorded in *Heimskringla*, when in 1151 in northern England, a raiding party defeated mounted knights and supporting infantry by their use of archery.

This reconstruction of a training session at Jomsborg shows the skjaldborg *arranged in a mutually supporting double line. Failure to maintain an arrow-proof defence could prove painful for the careless 'trainee'. A senior Jomsviking has chosen this moment to test the strength of the* skjaldborg *by attempting to kick one of the trainees out of position. (Gerry Embleton © Osprey Publishing Ltd)*

Despite the fact that they fought mostly on foot, the Vikings also occasionally fielded cavalry, as at the battle of Sulcoit in Ireland in 968, and at the battle of Montfaucon in France in 888, at which the chronicler Abbo of Fleury implies a large body of Viking cavalry was present, fighting separately from their infantry. More usually, however, they used horses simply as a means of increasing their mobility during their raiding expeditions. They either rounded up horses for this purpose in the vicinity of their encampment, or took those of the defeated enemy after a battle, as is recorded in the *Anglo-Saxon Chronicle* under the years 999 and 1010. In 866, a Viking force that had established a base in East Anglia obtained mounts and was able to go overland to York. No doubt the horses they brought with them to England from France in 885 and 892 had been similarly captured from defeated Frankish armies. In 885, the raising of the siege of Rochester led to the abandonment of the Vikings' horses. Loss of mobility may have influenced the departure to the Continent that followed.

A form of positional warfare developed in late 9th-century England with the Vikings and Saxons each making use of fortifications. These were often of

Reconstruction of a bridal found in a ship burial in Borre, Vestfold. (© Museum of Cultural History, University of Oslo, Norway, photographer Eirik Irgens Johnsen)

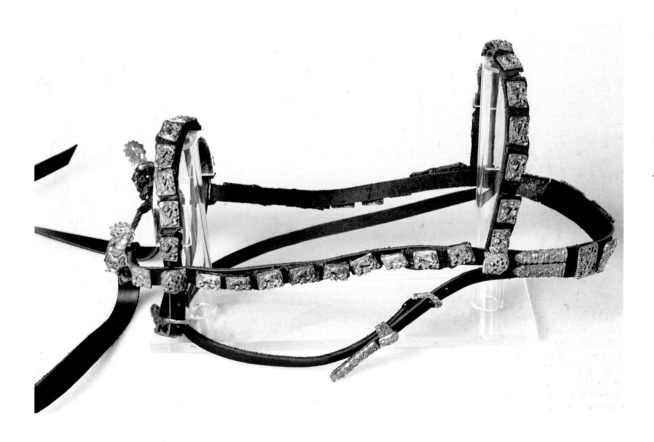

a temporary nature, unlike the Trelleborg forts of the Danish homelands (see 'Fortifications', page 106). Where they have been identified the Norse defences have always included a ditch and bank, and it seems likely that a wooden palisade would usually have been incorporated. The siege of Rochester in 885 may have involved the construction of lines of circumvallation. It is more probable that a less extensive fort was built outside the town's defences to act as a base for the Scandinavian attackers. In 894 King Alfred blockaded the two Viking camps at Appledore and Milton, acting as centres for raiding activities, and forced their abandonment. Remote coastal areas and islands were captured by the Vikings to provide safe havens. Such maritime bases were sometimes unfortified, relying on their remote location, surrounding water and Norse control of the seaways. Occupation of such sites was often temporary, although reuse in succeeding seasons was common.

Another feature of Scandinavian warfare still in evidence in the Viking Age was the 'hazelled field'. This was a specially chosen battlefield, fenced with hazel branches on all sides, where a battle was fought at a prearranged time and date by mutual agreement of the protagonists. Once challenged to fight in a hazelled field, it was apparently a dishonour to refuse or to ravage your opponent's territory until after the battle had been fought. The English were not unaware of this somewhat archaic tradition, since according to *Egil's Saga* the battle of Vinheidr, identified with the battle of Brunanburh in 937, took place in just such a hazelled field, which had been prepared by King Athelstan in order to delay the Vikings and their assorted Welsh and Scottish allies from pillaging until he had been able to assemble a large enough army to defeat them. The latest-known reference to such a hazelled field dates to 978, when Earl Hakon Sigurdsson of Norway defeated King Ragnfrid (one of Erik Bloodaxe's sons) in a field marked out with *hoslur*.

The Vikings also used much smaller-scale battle tactics. The deployment of fanatic units is discussed in the section on the battle of Hafrsfjord (page 110). Other specialists were also employed. At the battle of Svöldr, Olaf Tryggvasson had a bow-armed sniper, Einar Tambarskelf, on board his flagship. Missile-armed troops, while rarely deciding the course of an action, were almost always present. Many descriptions of battles include poetic euphemisms ('kennings') for arrows and throwing spears. The Old Norse language includes a word, *flyn*, specifically describing a throwing spear. Grettir Asmundson is said to have removed the rivet attaching the narrow head of a throwing spear to its shaft to prevent his intended victim from returning the missile.

Many weapons of the period would not necessarily be well suited to tight formations. Without room for manoeuvre, a long-handled axe swung with

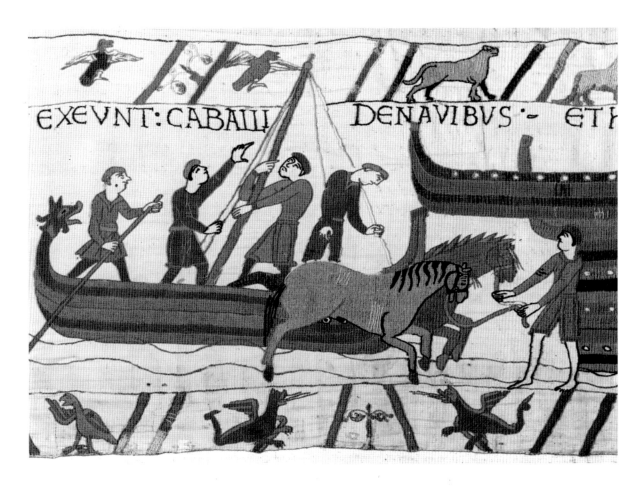

both hands is gravely handicapped. In the absence of surviving drill manuals, it seems reasonable to assume that units of Vikings were able to vary their formation according to circumstance. Egil and Thorolf Skallagrimson, while harrying Courland, split their forces into groups of 12 men. The Courlanders were unwilling to do more than skirmish with them, and Egil's unit unaided was able to assault a small settlement.

Horses being transported in Viking ships, as depicted in the Bayeux Tapestry. (R Sheridan / The Ancient Art & Architecture Collection Ltd)

Standards and signals

From the outset Viking armies had probably been accompanied by war flags (*gunnefanes*) bearing devices such as fanged, winged monsters: so at least we may suppose from the *Fulda Annals*' description of their standards as *signia horribilia*; and we know that even the Christian king Olaf Tryggvasson had a white standard bearing a serpent. However, the most widely recorded Viking standards were those bearing raven devices. Cnut, for instance, had a raven-embroidered white silk flag at the battle of Ashingdon in 1016, while the *Anglo-Saxon Chronicle*

Berserkers and Wolfcoats

In the pagan era, before Scandinavia was converted to Christianity, the *berserkir* were looked upon as possessing supernatural powers attributed to the Vikings' chief god, Odin. *Ynglinga Saga* records how in battle they 'rushed forward without armour, were as mad as dogs or wolves, bit their shields and were as strong as bears or wild boars, and killed people at a single blow, while neither fire nor iron could hurt them. This was called the berserk fury.' Today, we still refer to someone in a mad rage as having 'gone berserk'.

In reality this berserk fury was probably a form of paranoia, possibly related to a belief in lycanthropy, while in some cases it may even have been prompted by an epileptic attack. Whatever it was, it was clearly an hereditary condition rather than something that could be learnt. One account actually tells us that a particular man's 12 sons were all berserkers: 'It was their custom, if they were with their own men when they felt the berserk fury coming on, to go ashore and wrestle with large stones or trees; otherwise in their rage they would have slain their friends.'

Evidence for belief in lycanthropy can be found in *Volsunga Saga*, wherein we are told that Sigmund and his son Sinfjotli donned wolfskins, used the speech of wolves and howled when attacked; and in the legend of Hrolf Kraki, whose berserker champion, Bothvar Bjarki, reputedly fought in the likeness of a huge bear. Certainly wolves and bears are the animals most frequently associated with berserkers, for whom an alternative name was in fact *ulfhednar* ('wolfcoats' or 'wolfskin-clad ones'). This would seem to confirm beyond reasonable doubt that *berserkir* originally meant 'bear-shirt', and not 'bareshirt' as has so often been suggested.

The *Hrafnsmal* describes berserkers as men of great valour who never flinched in battle. This, along with the special favour with which Odin clearly regarded them, meant that they were to be found among the bodyguards of most pagan Viking kings, a troop of 12 being most commonly encountered in the sources. They fought in the forefront of every land battle and from the forecastle of the king's ship at sea. *Harald Fairhair's Saga* relates how on his ship 'the forecastle men were picked men for they had the king's banner. From the stem to the mid-hold was called the *rausn*, or the fore-defence; and there the berserkers were to be found. Such men only were received into King Harald's house-troop as were remarkable for strength, courage, and all kinds of dexterity; and they alone got a place in his ship.' It was probably berserkers to whom Snorri Sturlusson was referring in his description of the battle of Svöldr in 1000, where some men on King Olaf's ship forgot they were not fighting on land and 'rushed madly at the enemy, fell overboard and were drowned'.

In later Christian Iceland, the berserk fury was actually outlawed, and berserkers were regarded as some sort of ungodly fiend, whom the sagas represented as mindless bullies fit only to be cut down by an appropriate hero. It is possible that this attitude was also adopted in Christian Scandinavia.

records the capture of a standard actually called Reafan ('Raven') as early as 878. According to the *Annals of St Neot*, if 'Reafan' fluttered it signified a Viking victory, but if it drooped it meant a defeat.

A selection of Lewis chessmen. The one biting his shield presumably represents a berserker. The figure on the far right wears a vida stalhufa or 'wide steel hat', an early example of a kettle helmet. (CM Dixon/The Ancient Art & Architecture Collection Ltd)

Similar magical properties were attributed to the raven standard of Earl Sigurd of Orkney. It had been made for him by his mother, who was reputedly a sorceress, and is described as 'very cleverly embroidered in the shape of a raven, and when the banner fluttered in the breeze it seemed as if the raven spread its wings'. According to the *Orkneyinga Saga*, Sigurd's mother gave it to him with the warning that 'it will bring victory to the man it's carried before, but death to the one who carries it'. Sure enough, in the very first engagement in which it was carried Sigurd's standard-bearer was killed as soon as battle commenced: 'The earl told another man to pick up the banner but before long he was killed too. The earl lost three standard-bearers, but he won the battle.'

Some years later the same standard actually accompanied Earl Sigurd at the battle of Clontarf. *Njal's Saga* records the actions of Kerthjalfad, a foster-son of Irish High King Brian Boru:

[he] burst through Earl Sigurd's ranks right up to the banner, and killed the standard-bearer. The earl ordered someone else to carry the standard, and the

fighting flared up again. Kerthjalfad at once killed the new standard-bearer and all those who were near him. Earl Sigurd ordered Thorstein Hallsson to carry the standard, and Thorstein was about to take it when Amundi the White said, 'Don't take the banner, Thorstein. All those who bear it get killed.' 'Hrafn the Red,' said the earl, 'you take the standard.' 'Carry your own devil yourself,' said Hrafn. The earl then said, 'A beggar should carry his own bundle,' and he ripped the flag from its staff and tucked it under his clothing. A little later Amundi the White was killed, and then the earl himself died with a spear through him.

In the same way that Sigurd's raven standard was woven by his mother, the 'Reafan' standard captured by the Saxons in 878 is recorded to have been woven for the Danish commander there – a son of Ragnar Lodbrok (probably Ubbi) – by his own sisters. The undisguised implication was that they too must have been sorceresses, responsible for imbuing it with its victory-bringing powers. Indeed, the ability of a raven standard to impart victory was deep-rooted in pagan Scandinavian religion, since the raven was the bird of Odin and was associated with battlefield slaughter throughout the Germanic world. It

Hacksilver, coins and ingots from the Cuerdale hoard, possibly the paychest of a Viking army. The change from plunder to regular payment in such silver 'monetary specie' brought one of the greatest differences in the character of the Viking warrior towards the end of the Viking period. (HIP/The British Museum/Topfoto)

therefore seems likely that Harald Hardrada's flag Landeythan ('Landwaster') similarly bore a raven, since it 'was said to bring victory to the man before whom it was borne in battle – and that had been so ever since he got it'. Even as late as King Sverri of Norway's reign (1184–1202) we read, in *Sverri's Saga*, of a lenderman saying: 'Let us hoist the standard before the king … and let us hew a sacrifice beneath the raven's talons.'

In addition to standards, commanders used various other signals to communicate with their men. *Egil's Saga* mentions the use of horns for signalling instructions to the dispersed sections of pillagers in the Courland incident. We also read of signal calls for arming, to put to sea, to land, to attack and advance. Trumpets are also used to summon general assemblies in settlements. Such a variety of applications suggests that these signals were widely understood.

The sagas credit several outstanding Scandinavian generals of the early Middle Ages with a series of unlikely ploys and stratagems. These are folk-tales of unusual persistence often attached to the name of more than one leader. They range from feigned death, to gain entry to a besieged city claiming the need for burial, to the highly dubious use of wild birds as unwitting incendiaries. Even if none of these stories are true, they represent an interest in disinformation and trickery which would not shame more systematic students of warfare.

Conventional forms of surprise attack were used. The winter assault on the Wessex royal palace at Chippenham was a master stroke that caught Alfred off his guard with almost fatal consequences. We see the Vikings mounting an offensive during a time when their enemy could reasonably expect them to be inactive – during a religious festival, from an unexpected direction, using speed and overwhelming force. This has all the ingredients of an ideal surprise attack. It can be seen that without the benefit of formal military institutions the oral traditions of the Viking warrior still provided him with a range of strategic and tactical options.

LOGISTICS

Equipping and supplying a Viking army was a vastly different undertaking in the 8th century than it was later in the period. During the earlier part of the Viking Age decentralized power was unable to raise large forces without the consent of local warlords.

These need not have been any more powerful than the *hersir*. Regional forces would have been raised and equipped within their own area of habitation. The later laws (*Hirdskra*) for the defence of Norway on a territorial basis are a late survival of this. The clan and tribe would each play their part in making it possible to mount an expedition. Organization of war effort would rest with local landowners, who would also be the leaders of society.

The semi-legendary Ragnar Lodbrok, who was the leader of the earliest manifestation of the Great Army in England, appears to have laid claim to royal status. It would seem that, as with the ancient clan system, the reality of power lay with his *aett*. As mentioned previously, the 'sons of Lodbrok' (who may not have been blood relatives) were said to have conquered the northern kingdoms of the heptarchy in revenge for their 'father' having been executed in Northumbria. The Great Army worked on a series of interlocking loyalties that were not immutable. The campaigns of the army show that smaller groups were at liberty to conduct minor operations. One of the Lodbroksons was killed while raiding Devon in 878. The aim of this attack may have been to obtain land for settlement; in 876 Halfdan had divided Northumbria amongst his followers. It is equally possible that the assault of 878 was intended as a *strandhögg*.

Two different systems of logistics can be seen at work. The opportunistic raiders established control of land and agriculture in the political vacuum of Northumbria. In the future, the Norse kings of York were to have a troubled but effective reign which, with some interruptions, continued until the mid-10th century. Armies were raised and equipped from this area, sometimes supported by overseas Vikings. The 878 incident may have had more important implications, but the form of attack was that which had surprised Lindisfarne in 793, a swift descent on an unprotected coast. The invaders would take whatever they needed from the region and move on. Unfortunately for their leader (according to the *Annals of St Neot* he was Hubba Lodbrokson), the nature of the defence had changed. Although the king of Wessex was himself a fugitive, the local ealdorman was capable of meeting and destroying Hubba without assistance from the central state. Ealdormen were unlike the minor kings of the earlier period with a personal connection to their region, but were royal officials who could be appointed, dismissed or transferred. The outcome might reflect the vagaries of warfare, but some level of preparedness must have been necessary to defeat a force of 23 ships.

Fortifications

The militarization of the English state, which made the defeat of the raiders and the conquest of England possible, depended on the network of fortifications that the Wessex dynasty was to build in the late 9th and 10th centuries. Positional warfare became more important in the later part of Alfred's reign as the Scandinavians attempted to defend their gains and break the last Saxon kingdom. The *Burghal Hideage* gives a picture of the way in which

Aerial view of Trelleborg military camp, thought to have been constructed as troop assembly points for Swein Forkbeard's operations against England. It was well protected on three sides by rivers and a marsh, and with man-made defences including a stockaded rampart. (National Museum of Denmark)

Reconstruction of Trelleborg military camp. Four gates in the ramparts linked to roads dividing the area into four equal sectors, each containing four principal buildings arranged in squares. In addition, there were a further 15 houses in the outer ward. (National Museum of Denmark)

royal foundations were established every 20 miles or so. Supported by the resources of their area, these were concentrations of regal power where mints, markets and refuge defences could be placed. The *burh* could act as a centre of control and resistance or as a base for further operations. In England these were often raised on the site of existing settlements, sometimes augmenting or adapting urban foundations of Roman origin. This phase of primary state formation has left similar traces in the archaeology of Scandinavia.

The most developed of the Viking kingdoms, Denmark, saw the building of a remarkable series of regional fortresses in the 9th century. These are named after the site of Trelleborg, although the earliest of the group appears to be the one at Fyrkat. The surprising regularity of their ground plan has led some writers to surmise that the Trelleborg forts were built to a strict military plan. Some have even suggested a modified 'Roman foot' in the measurement of the fortifications. This is about as likely as the completely bogus 'pyramid inch'. In fact these defensive works are not as innovative as they may first appear to be. The circular outline of the fortresses could be marked out with nothing more complex than a long rope attached at a single fixed point. Circular refuge forts of earlier date are known from the Baltic Åland Islands and from the Low Countries. The regularity of the internal buildings may reflect short-term occupation rather than a strictly military function. Interpretations that date these structures to the reign of Swein Forkbeard or Cnut have stressed the military origin.

There can be little doubt that the Trelleborg forts were the product of a strong monarchy. They may even have been inspired by the *burh* system of Anglo-Saxon England. The purpose they served was the same — control of a developing country. The Danish conquest of England in the early 11th century was almost certainly made possible by the well-organized logistic infrastructure provided by the Trelleborg forts of Denmark.

Recruitment

The changing nature of the Viking warrior is exemplified by the shift from the regional method of recruitment and supply to the more complex national system. The crucial role of kings in this can be seen by the increasing importance of royalty in major projects. One of the largest longships ever built in the north was the *Long Serpent* funded by Olaf Tryggvasson, who also contributed to the design. The logistics that supported the new, cohesive armies developed in some senses from the gift economy; hence Tryggvasson at the battle of Svöldr is seen issuing swords to his bodyguard. One characteristic of good lordship in this period was the bestowal of fitting weapons.

The Jomsvikings were early participants in the Danegeld bonanza at the turn of the 10th and 11th centuries. Their main aim was the extortion of silver coinage. Thorkell the Tall had no inhibitions about changing sides as long as the flow of silver to his men was not interrupted. This was in fact their pay, and although the financial practices of the age still tend to treat weight and quality of silver as the true value, the step to a currency based on confidence was only a short one. This immature version of economics was sufficient to support professional units like the Jomsvikings who could devote all their time to warfare.

The problem of supply was relatively simple for a Viking force. When not equipping in the homelands for an expedition, they lived off the land by plunder, extorting directly from established authorities or settling in the lands they had destabilized. Transportation of supplies does not appear to have been by cart. Surviving examples of wheeled transport from Scandinavia are ceremonial and of a construction that could not have withstood extended use in a land of virtually non-existent roads. Written records from Iceland contain copious references to pack-horses.

Viking fort, AD 950–1000. This Danish fortress, typical of the 'Trelleborg' series, features the precise layout of the main hall structures, arranged in fours around the side of a square. Each group of four is positioned within a quadrant of the characteristic circular rampart. Like all known sites of this type the fort is situated near a great water feature. The emergence of such structures was a feature of growing royal power in Denmark. (Gerry Embleton © Osprey Publishing Ltd)

THE VIKINGS IN BATTLE
The battle of Hafrsfjord *c.* 872

The only written records of the battle appear in Icelandic literature and were probably first composed over 200 years after the events described. However, the various sagas that touch upon the engagement are generally agreed in outline and details. The importance of Hafrsfjord in Icelandic history lies in the impetus to emigration which followed the unfavourable outcome.

The forces engaged were those of Harald Harfagri, the would-be sole king of Norway, and a loose alliance of landowners of varying social standing from the northern and western areas of the country.

Harald Harfagri was the son of Halfdan the Black and through his father had inherited the minor kingdom of Vestfold. This area was of some importance as a trade route dominating the southern approaches to Norway (Kaupang was the principal entrepôt of the region). The large amount of level, fertile land around

The battlefield of Hafrsfjord, c. 872. Onund Treefoot is about to earn his nickname at the hands of an axe-armed Ulfhednar. While defending himself from a spear thrust during a boarding attempt, the hero has 'blind-sided' himself with his own shield. (Gerry Embleton © Osprey Publishing Ltd)

the Vik gave Harald certain advantages over his rivals. By a process of isolating and eliminating the petty kings of Norway one at a time, Harald had succeeded in absorbing or subduing Uppland, Trondelag, Naumdale, Halogaland, Maera and Raumsdale. If *Egil's Saga* is to be believed, many people had already been forced into exile by the growing power of Harald. Of those who remained, 'many great men' resolved to rebel against Harald in defence of their right to unattached landholdings. They were supported in this by the still independent King Sulki of

Rogaland. *Grettir's Saga* informs us that Geirmund Swathyskin, the overlord of Hjordaland, one of the few remaining independent kingdoms, was absent overseas. The names of additional allied leaders were Kjotvi the Wealthy and Thorir Longchin (the deposed king of Agdir).

Although Hafrsfjord took place at sea, it bore little resemblance to a true naval action. Projectile weapons played little part in the course of the fight, which was resolved by a series of boarding actions. Neither was deliberate ramming in the pattern of classical naval warfare a tactic employed at this time.

The precise size and composition of the two forces is not known, although Icelandic sources describe this as the largest battle ever fought by King Harald. *Egil's Saga* makes a particular point of listing the 'forecastle' men on King Harald's ship, as these were to play an important part. Among them was the retained Thorolf Kvendulfson, the brother of Skallagrim Kveldulfson and uncle of Egil. The group of hand-picked warriors in the prow of the ship appears to have been deployed behind an even more select group of berserkers. *Egil's Saga* gives the number of the king's berserkers as 12, a figure that recurs in Norse literature when groups of these unusual warriors appear.

The intention of the king was to come alongside the ship of Thorir Longchin and strike directly at one of the foremost leaders of the allied force. King Harald ordered forward his Wolfskins, on whom no iron could bite and whose charge nothing could resist. Thorir Longchin was cut down in the onset. His followers' resolve collapsed, giving King Harald the victory.

Stripping this key section of the battle of any mystical elements, we can see that a centralizing monarchy is able to raise, equip and maintain a specialist fighting unit whose reputation is supernatural. At the crucial moment they are sent forward with a definite target whose elimination will cause the collapse of the opposition. Harald Harfagri's tactics might be relatively simple, but the result was to influence the entire history of Norway and the very nature of the Viking warrior.

Brunanburh or Vinheath *c.* 937

The image of the leader as the generous donor of valuables to his loyal followers remained one of the governing concepts of the early Middle Ages. Men fought not only for honour and glory but also for immediate and fitting reward. The form of such gifts might vary depending on the status of the recipient. To the young warrior of the immediate *hearth-weru*, or bodyguard, movable wealth, preferably in the form of ornamental jewellery, would be appropriate. One of the poetic descriptions of a good lord was 'ring-giver'. To an established noble or older veteran the right to land might be more

11th-century carved head in elk-horn, wearing a decorated conical helmet with nasal, from Sigtuna, Uppland, Sweden. (Topfoto)

important. As the gift economy changed towards one based on silver coinage, a mercenary class seems to have emerged. The story of Egil Skallagrimson at Brunanburh reflects several aspects of this change.

Although the Wessex kings had established their supremacy over the lowlands, the peripheral areas of Britain, and in particular those under Celtic

or Norse cultural domination, had not abandoned hope of independence. The similarity of Athelstan's position to that of Harald Harfagri in 872 is striking. That some fellow feeling, or at least a commonality of interest, existed between the two is shown by Athelstan's fostering of Hakon, the son of Harald.

The broad anti-English alliance had made strange political bedfellows of several lesser kings whose domains encircled the Irish Sea. These included Olaf, the king of Dublin, a man of mixed Norse and Celtic descent who, according to *Egil's Saga*, was the prime mover of the allies.

The collapse of the accord of 927 between Athelstan and the northern kings began when the allies appear to have invaded Northumbria. The extent of their penetration into Saxon territory is unclear. Following the defeat of the joint Northumbrian earls Gudrek and Alfgeir, some form of harrying inside the northern part of Athelstan's realm seems to have taken place. To counter this, Athelstan issued a challenge to the allies to meet within a defined area to decide who ruled Britain by combat. After such a challenge, it was considered dishonourable to plunder further. Athelstan, in his preparations for a northward march, had sent word throughout north-western Europe that he wished to hire mercenaries. Egil Skallagrimson and his brother Thorolf had been made aware of this while in the Low Countries and, we are told, were singled out by the king as suitable generals for the entire mercenary force. The part played by the hired warriors in this fight receives no mention in the *Chronicle* account, which instead highlights the contribution of the West Saxon and Mercian contingents.

Egil's Saga stresses the experiences of the Skallagrimson brothers in the fight and how their professional code determines everything from their equipment to the way in which they confront death. They are described as particularly well equipped both with defensive armour and specialized mail-piercing weapons. The fulfilment of their agreement with the king leads them into the thickest part of the battle where Thorolf and his men are abandoned by a Saxon earl named Alfgeir. In spite of this, Thorolf is able to fight his way out of encirclement, cutting down Hring, the Strathclyde British general, in the process. Resistance from the allied army continues and during a lull in the fighting Athelstan gives his personal thanks to the Skallagrimsons. The saga theme of never trusting a king asserts itself. Athelstan insists on a faulty disposition of his troops, leading to the death of Thorolf, cut down in a surprise attack launched from a wood by the men of Strathclyde.

The survivors of Thorolf's personal unit are forced back, but galvanized by the appearance of Egil in their ranks they rally, counterattack and put the

OPPOSITE *The battle of Brunanburh. In the foreground opposing skjaldborgr are meeting in an onset of two swine arrays. Employing a combination of spears and secondary weapons, the two aetts are attempting to push back or kill their opponents and penetrate the enemy formation. The battlefield was the ultimate test of the bonds of kinship, artificial or otherwise, within a warrior group. (Gerry Embleton © Osprey Publishing Ltd)*

115

Strathclyde contingent to flight. In the process, the remaining Strathclyde British leader Adils is killed. The personal nature of the relationship between leaders and followers is revealed by the rout of the Strathclyde British on the demise of their overlord. The death of Adils (as with the death of Thorir Longchin at Hafrsfjord) leads to the end of the obligation to fight. The professionalism of Thorolf's unit allows it to conduct a fighting withdrawal.

The final act of Brunanburh for the saga writer is the confrontation between Egil and King Athelstan. In the story, the Saxon king represents the principle that sacrifices all for power. The clan of Kveldulf was divided into two characteristic types of dark and fair Maera-men. Thorolf, as a representative of the latter type, was susceptible to the glamour surrounding royalty. Egil, one of the dark Maera-men, retained the scepticism of an earlier independent age. Thorolf's trust had brought him to his death, and Egil now sought redress for the loss to his clan.

After an effective and bloody pursuit, Egil returned to bury his brother on the battlefield with due solemnity and two poems, one on the glory of Thorolf and the sorrow occasioned by his death and another on Egil's personal triumphs. Duty fulfilled, the surviving brother returned to the king's headquarters, where a celebratory feast was underway. According to the saga, Athelstan made arrangements for Egil to be seated in a place of honour, but this was clearly insufficient to the son of Skallagrim who sat fully equipped and scowling. Eventually, when the king restored the balance of respect and recognition by passing to the bereaved warrior a gold arm-ring (symbolically presented on the point of a sword) Egil felt able to take off his armour and join the festivities.

Maldon 991

The greatest Old English battle poem is an untitled piece on the death of Byhrtnoth, the ealdorman of Essex. Not only is this the major source for the events of the battle of Maldon but it also provides the clearest statement of the Germanic heroic ideal. Historically, the battle sealed the fate of the Saxon kingdom and began a train of events that was to lead to the destruction of the Wessex dynasty.

By the end of the 10th century, the Scandinavian invaders had not won a battle in England for over a hundred years. The independence of the Danelaw had been eroded in a series of devastating campaigns, and a network of *burhs* was established to maintain centralized control. Attempts by a joint Viking army to break the Saxon position in Essex had centred on a siege of the fortification at Maldon in 925. The arrival of a relief force had prevented the

fall of the town, and the front line of the Saxon resurgence moved further north to the kingdom of York, where Norse penetration had been more complete. By the year of the second battle of Maldon, the Saxon domination of the lowland zone of Britain was total. The kingdom had been divided into areas of subordinate authority, each controlled by an ealdorman. One of these was Byhrtnoth, a man of noble family who was initially the Ealdorman of East Anglia but subsequently moved to the less important posting of Essex in his advanced age.

In the 980s, Viking raiders again appeared off the coast of England. These were not led by the minor chieftains of a displaced Norwegian nobility or land-hungry farmers from overcrowded Scandinavia. They were a mixed band of freebooters seeking immediate and large gains in silver. The exhaustion of the Central Asian silver mines had led to the collapse of the Russian trade routes and the necessity to introduce a new source of wealth to Viking spheres of

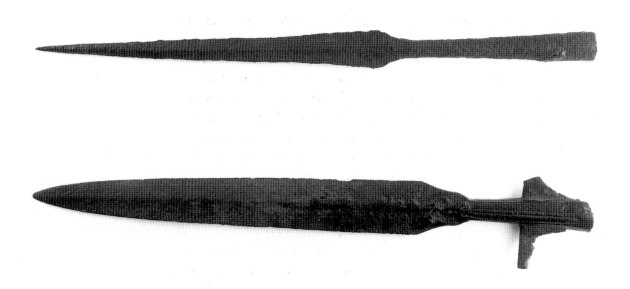

influence. Interestingly, the leaders of the new wave of Viking attacks included men like Thorkell the Tall (one of the captains of the semi-professional Jomsvikings) and Olaf Tryggvasson (the pretender to the throne of Norway), both men who needed money to further their ambitions at home.

The revived raids on eastern England in the summer of 991 differed from the small scale of affairs of previous decades. Major cities, like Ipswich, now became viable targets for large raiding armies. The Vikings at Maldon were said to have deployed a fleet of 93 ships, although the exact size of the invading army cannot be inferred from this as the number of men in a ship's crew is not known. The estimates are in the region of several thousand warriors.

The defending forces under Byhrtnoth included his own personal bodyguard, probably a fairly large unit as the ealdorman's career had been long and successful and his popularity sufficient to persuade men to fight on after the normal bonds of agreement demanded. The local levy, or *fyrd*, was also present in large numbers. Maldon was a local centre of sufficient importance to house a royal mint, and the area of Essex would have been mobilized by the threat of the Vikings. The training and morale of the *fyrd* was of variable quality but generally low. This lack of expertise and dedication was to prove disastrous.

After plundering Ipswich, the Vikings rounded the Tendring peninsula and entered the estuary of the Blackwater. They established themselves on the island of Northey, in the time-honoured manner of Vikings on a hostile coast, and although the *burh* at Maldon appears to have defied or missed their attentions they were firmly in position when Byhrtnoth arrived to take up position on the landward side of Northey's tidal causeway.

That both protagonists were eager to give battle would perhaps indicate an equality of forces. Byhrtnoth's motivations in bringing the pirates to battle may have included a desire to prevent them escaping to ravage other areas or even a genuine belief that the forces facing him could be defeated by his own command. The poem makes it clear that the ealdorman was in full and effective control of his force from the start, when he gives instructions to his noble followers to release their hawks and drive away their horses. The poet appears to be saying that beasts were free to depart the place of slaughter but that men, bound by honour and obligation, must remain.

The defence of the causeway

Within the poem of the battle we are given a literary interpretation of the course of an early medieval engagement. A messenger from the Viking host brings Byhrtnoth a demand from his leaders which can be summarized as a demand for money with menaces. The ealdorman hotly rejects this in an answer that forges the ideas of loyalty (in this case to King Ethelred), national pride and a personal refusal to be intimidated into a response that invites the Norsemen to do their worst. Having rejected blackmail, Byhrtnoth now commits his forces to a desperate engagement that resolves itself into three sections. The first is an exchange of missiles across the tidal creek which separates Northey from the mainland, developing into a defence of the causeway access by three champions. The literal truth of all this might be difficult to prove, and it should be borne in mind that the poet was probably influenced by the classical story of 'Horatius on the Bridge'. Attempts to rationalize this phase of the poem's narrative have included the interpretation of the three Saxon heroes as the commanders of sub-units detailed to an important post.

Failing to break the Saxon position on the narrow land-bridge, the 'heathens' again send a messenger who asks that the battle should be continued on the mainland. In agreeing to this request Byhrtnoth opens himself to accusations by the poet of being overly courageous (though the word *ofermod* may not imply foolhardiness). Like the battle of Brunanburh, the fight at Maldon might have been governed by conventions only dimly understood today. The ealdorman's wish to force a conclusion led to the 'pagans' being allowed to cross to a more convenient site on the land and the continuation of the struggle. As the English came under increasing pressure, they began to lose heart, and Byhrtnoth's mistake in putting his horse in the charge of one Godric proved disastrous when Godric mounted and fled. The levy of Essex mistook Godric for the ealdorman himself, and behaved accordingly.

The isolated bodyguard was now at the mercy of the Vikings, and again we see the tactics of an all-out attack on the supreme commander. Byhrtnoth is struck by a thrown javelin. In death, Byhrtnoth's thoughts were on refuge with a Christian God as much as glory. His household troop resolved to end fighting around the body of their lord. (The laws of the Jomsvikings included a similar refusal to give ground, but allowed for retreat if faced by overwhelming odds.)

The subsequent action of King Ethelred in paying ever-increasing sums of Danegeld to Scandinavian invaders was as much a response to the entire late 10th-century wave of attacks as the single defeat of Maldon. The payments were to fund the national invasions of the early 11th century under the Danish kings. The Anglo-Norse elite that emerged from this period based much of its military power on a version of the household warrior bands typified by the Royal Huscarls of Harold Godwinsson who were to fight and die at Hastings.

MOTIVATION AND PSYCHOLOGY

The earliest references to the warrior ideals of the Germanic races can be found in the work of classical authors from Strabo onwards. The sacrifice of the fruits of victory by ritual destruction is to be seen in Danish bog deposits of the Iron Age and is described in the *Universal History* of Orosius. Sacrifice is recognized as the fulfilment of specific vows, something the Graeco-Roman world was perfectly familiar with. Captured wealth, equipment and prisoners were dedicated to the gods in return for assistance in winning battles. The conviction that the battlefield was the province of a powerful warrior deity survived among the Nordic people long after the conversion to Christianity of the more southerly Germanic tribes of the Continent.

The name of the Scandinavian battle god is not always the same, being concealed by euphemisms and metaphorical titles. At least two alternative war gods existed as detailed by the Icelandic writer Snorri Sturlusson. These were Tyr, a specialized battle god, and Odin, the father of the gods and a more complex figure whose areas of interest extended to all aspects of power politics (see 'Religion', page 35).

Violence as a way of life remained part of the Scandinavian ethos until well into the Middle Ages, when Christianity was long established. It is not possible to explain away the whole of Scandinavian warfare by references to the battle gods. In many ways the god was a symptom of a violent culture rather than the cause of it.

If Sturlusson's account can be believed, the Viking warrior found his fitting home in the 'Hall of the Slain', Valhalla. Here Odin presided over the ultimate expression of the gift economy, providing the chosen with all that was good on an unbelievably lavish scale and the benefit of fighting to the death with daily resurrections. Odin's recruitment of warriors might be justified in early medieval pagan terms by the argument that the larger the warband the more powerful the leader. The motive given by Sturlusson has further implications. Odin is raising an army of super-warriors to fight at the apocalyptic battle of Ragnarok. This sounds suspiciously like the later medieval interpretation of the place of the human soul in heaven. The Christian God is recruiting perfected souls to replace the fallen angels. However, Sturlusson was a Christian writing for a Christian audience. It is not

A 12th-century tapestry detail illustrating the struggle between Christianity and paganism. The three figures to the right are ringing bells to frighten away evil spirits and pagan gods. (Werner Forman Archive/Statens Historiska Museet, Stockholm)

even certain that the average Viking even believed in Sturlusson's version of Valhalla. The extent to which his descriptions of Norse religion reflect reality can never now be fully assessed as no pagan version of the Norse myths survives for comparison.

The conceptual cosmos of the Viking warrior might be bounded at the supernatural level by a final fight alongside a generous and worthy lord. The earthly world was governed by essentially the same concept. The lord in early Germanic society was a crucial figure around whom society revolved. The origin of the word in the Old English *Hlaf-ord* ('Loaf ward'), the controller of bread, gives us a clue to this central position. In a primitive farming community, the man who dominated the distribution of food was the effective ruler. It was this idea of a ruling figure that was to evolve first into an extended local lordship and finally into the monarchy. As the nature of power changed, the attitudes of the warrior changed as well.

The nature of leadership

Ganga Hrolf, a son of Jarl Rognvald of Moer, found himself exiled from Norway for breaking the ban on raiding within Harald Harfagri's realm. Ganga and his followers operated along the Seine in the early part of the 10th

Viking warrior, 8th–9th centuries. This warrior is of the hersir *class at the height of the Nordic threat to Europe. His status is distinguished by his ownership of helmet, gold arm-ring and decorated sword. Non-Christian beliefs are revealed by the hammer-shaped amulet. (Gerry Embleton © Osprey Publishing Ltd)*

century and ultimately dominated it to such an extent that the Frankish monarchy was forced to cede the future duchy of Normandy to them. During the negotiations with the Franks, an often-quoted exchange occurred as recorded by Dudo of St Quentin. When questioned as to the authority of their leader, they replied that he had no authority as all were equal. This may be simply an evasive answer, but we know from the later history of the duchy that Rolf, or Rollo, was in fact the leader of this group. The nature of leadership amongst the earlier raiding parties is somewhat unclear. The bands of Vikings operating in north-western Europe between the end of the 8th century and the end of the 10th century appear to have joined together or separated as circumstance required.

Long-term commitment did not extend beyond the immediate leader of a warrior's group, who might very probably be a native of one's own region if not a near relative. This form of close-knit group gains certain obvious advantages. Unity of purpose is liable to be stronger. In battle, the unit will act in a more cohesive and mutually supportive way, and the abandoning of wounded comrades is less likely.

Good commanders commonly toured their armies immediately prior to battle to make sure that all was ready for action. Encouraging speeches were made to strengthen the resolve of the combatants, and sometimes poetry was composed on the spot. This showed not only the sophistication of the poet but also his composure, a quality that would hopefully be transmitted to his followers.

Extreme behaviour during battle was commonplace. Such actions might be based in a religion that glorified the warrior and made the prerequisite for a suitable afterlife the display of superlative fighting qualities. Sagas abound with desperate engagements where the main motivation of the participant is not mere survival. A man who faced odds was testing his own worth, and at the same time, his luck against his enemies.

Strength of purpose was another Viking trait. While Erik Bloodaxe was enjoying his brief and unpopular reign in Norway, Egil Skallagrimson had fallen foul of Queen Gunnhilda. The king had ordered Egil's death, but the Icelander had shown himself too elusive for the tyrant. Trapped on an island by the royal retainers who were carefully guarding all boats, Egil stripped his equipment. Making a bundle of his sword, helmet and spear (less the shaft, discarded to create a handier weapon) he swam to a nearby islet. As the search for him widened, a small boat with 12 fighting men landed on his refuge where he was keeping careful watch. Nine of the party went inland, and Egil attacked the remainder, making use of the local terrain and a sudden assault. Cutting down one man in the first onset, he sliced the foot from a second who tried to flee up a slope. The survivor was attempting to pole off the boat when Egil seized a trailing rope and hauled his prey in. No single Norwegian was ever a match for Egil at the height of his strength, and the victim was soon despatched. The implication is clear: two of Egil's opponents were killed because their nerve had failed them. Egil, however, had maintained his presence of mind and with tremendous strength of purpose evaded the might of King Erik.

The kind of resolve and immediate action that characterized Egil's behaviour is consistently held up in Norse literature as the role model for the warrior. The *Hávamál*, the mythical advice of Odin to mankind (quoted on page 40), contains a series of verses stressing the virtue of careful consideration and attack. This theme, in its oral form, was one of the major influences on the mind of the Viking *hersir*.

APPEARANCE AND EQUIPMENT

The earliest large-scale seaborne raid of Scandinavians on Europe was that conducted by the Geats under Hygelac. The leaders of this southern Swedish tribe can be expected to have carried equipment comparable to that found in the elite status graves of Valsgarde and Vendel. The panoplies yielded by these sites are similar to those discovered at Sutton Hoo in Suffolk. The Valsgarde garniture included a set of armour far more extensive than any we have evidence for in the Viking period proper. By the end of the 8th century, the splinted limb armour of the Valsgarde chieftain appears to have fallen out of use. Arguments have been made for the re-emergence of such items in the Byzantine-influenced armour of the Varangian Guard. However, equipment such as this can never have been widespread and was probably of little value in mobile warfare. The warriors who descended on Lindisfarne were almost certainly less well fitted out. Even the war-gear of a local leader would not have been so complete as that of his 7th-century predecessor. This reduction of armament would appear to correspond to a change in the nature of war as practised by the Vikings. Territorial battles in the homelands were no longer the only profitable outlet for Scandinavian energies. More mobile forms of war would require the warrior to be more lightly equipped.

Clothing and grooming

Observers in the early Middle Ages comment on the great care Norsemen took over their general appearance. The number of combs found on Viking sites show a deep concern for grooming. The well-coiffured head on the Sigtuna elk-antler carving, with its impressive handlebar moustache, shows this to be more than just an interest in delousing. Personal hygiene 'kits', some highly decorative, have been found in both male and female graves. These include tweezers for plucking superfluous hair and tiny spoons for removing ear-wax. Only a person of status could afford to spend time on such activities. Consequently a well-turned-out appearance would be the hallmark of the warrior of middle or high rank.

Dressing for war was not so much a matter of uniform or camouflage as an expression of wealth and pride. The warrior would appear in his finest and most conspicuous clothing. In *Njal's Saga*, Skarphedin dresses before violent encounters in the most ostentatious fashion. Participants in feuds are recognized at a distance by characteristic items of apparel. The intention often appears to be the advertisement rather than concealment of their presence.

Shoes and boots were constructed of leather or hide usually obtained from cattle but sometimes from seals or reindeer. The ancient name for a hide shoe was *hriflingr*. The *hersir* might be expected to wear more elegant footwear of dressed skin like those found in Hungate and Coppergate in York. Boots and shoes were made in a variety of styles. They could be cut from a single piece of leather or made up from two sections stitched along a vamp — a seam running along the upper towards the toe of the shoe. Soles were usually made from separate pieces of leather. Footwear could be in other than natural colours: Skarphedin, for example, had a black pair. A sock was discovered at Coppergate knitted of woollen yarn, but apparently not shaped to allow for the heel and toes.

Trousers of varying fullness were worn in the 7th to 9th centuries. The Gotland gravestones and the tapestries from Skogg and Oseberg show them as baggy and gathered anywhere from mid-calf to just below the knee. The Gotland gravestones show clearly that they were worn in combat. The Oseberg tapestry depicts the same full trousers as the dress of the high-status warrior. Tight-fitting trousers became more fashionable in the 10th and 11th centuries. This may be due to Scandinavian exposure to English and Continental fashion. By the early 11th century, King Cnut is shown wearing close-fitting hose or stockings. These seem to be bound around the mid-leg with strips or garters of decorated material below which the fitting appears to be somewhat wrinkled.

Comb decorated with a human and animal head. The comb is pre-Viking. Similar combs have been found on Viking sites. (Werner Forman Archive / Statens Historiska Museet, Stockholm)

A whalebone plaque from a boat burial in Sanday, Orkney. Such plaques were often used for smoothing linen clothing. (R Thorne/The Ancient Art & Architecture Collection Ltd)

Trousers were made either of linen or woven wool. Other constructional details are lost as the various contemporary depictions do not show seams.

Tunics

Representations of tunics from the first two centuries of the Viking Age show knee-length garments with full skirts gathered at the waist, usually by a belt. There is little change until the later part of the period. The neck of the tunic could be square or round, and was fastened by a drawstring, garment hook, or

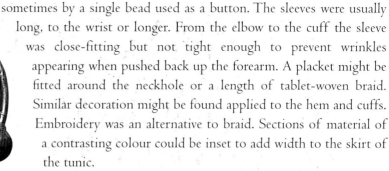

sometimes by a single bead used as a button. The sleeves were usually long, to the wrist or longer. From the elbow to the cuff the sleeve was close-fitting but not tight enough to prevent wrinkles appearing when pushed back up the forearm. A placket might be fitted around the neckhole or a length of tablet-woven braid. Similar decoration might be found applied to the hem and cuffs. Embroidery was an alternative to braid. Sections of material of a contrasting colour could be inset to add width to the skirt of the tunic.

The colours used on the Bayeux Tapestry are a good guide to those available in the Viking period. Dyeing technology is not likely to have changed radically before the end of the 11th century. The impressive permanence of the Bayeux colours suggests the use of an effective (and presumably expensive) mordant. There is no reason that such materials would not have been available in Scandinavia by import, if not by indigenous production. Undyed material was probably widely used by the poor, although Vikings of higher status would favour more colourful attire.

Cloaks of rectangular or square shape appear to have been the norm; they can be seen worn by warriors, though not usually in combat. They were held at the shoulders by a brooch or pin. Embroidered cloaks are also mentioned in the sagas. Hoods could be improvised by folding the cloaks or possibly added to the garment as separate pieces of material.

Relics of civilian headgear, which would have been worn when helmets were inappropriate, include the fur-trimmed hat from Birka which was influenced by Eastern fashions. The detached hood of red-brown tabby-weave silk found in the Coppergate dig is assumed to be an item of female dress, although the main argument for this appears to be a photograph of the item being worn by a female researcher. Hats of felt are described in several sagas, and Odin is said to have worn a broad-brimmed version as part of a disguise.

Other dress accessories (which might also be worn in battle) include leather belts with decorated buckles and strap ends. Belts were usually narrow, less than 1 inch (2.5 centimetres) wide. Belt fittings were mostly of copper alloy; examples carved in bone and painted in verdigris were less common. Additional equipment could include a leather pouch. Purses were often of the type cut as a thin disc of leather closed by a drawstring looped through holes in the rim. A larger version of this, the *nestbaggin*, acted as a haversack for the campaigning *hersir*.

Helmets

The only helmet that can be definitely ascribed to the Vikings is one found at Gjermundbu, and is usually dated to the later 9th century. In outward appearance it follows the earlier tradition of Scandinavian helmets, having a fixed visor of the characteristic 'spectacle' form. However, there are considerable differences in structure. The Gjermundbu helmet is formed by a brow band, a skeleton of two metal bars and four shaped plates which make up the dome. One of the bars is aligned along the centre of the skull and the other across the bowl from ear to ear. Both bars are attached to the brow band as is the fixed visor. The four sections of the dome are rivetted to the cross pieces to fill the spaces between the various components. The pre-Viking Valsgarde and Vendel helmets are altogether more elaborate. Some of them have an additional reinforcing crest or *wala*, others cheek pieces. The helmets of the true Viking Age have more in common with the Gjermundbu specimen.

A carved elk-antler from Sigtuna in Sweden depicts a warrior wearing a conical helmet. This appears to be of four shaped plates held together by rivets. Although it shows no sign of any structural members, a row of rivets around

OPPOSITE *Helmet from a 7th-century Vendel boat grave. Although this predates the Vikings and has a more elaborate design, the 'spectacle'-like face guard and nosepiece are features of later Viking helmets. (Werner Forman Archive/Statens Historiska Museet, Stockholm)*

the base of the helmet indicates the presence of at least a brow band. A nasal extension shown on this piece might be interpreted as a projection of the longitudinal skull band, though this is not certain. Viking monumental art, for example the Kirlevington, Sockburn and Middleton cross fragments, show figures wearing what are probably conical helmets but could equally be pointed caps or hoods. The Weston Church cross fragment shows a bare-headed warrior.

Two famous helmets from Central Europe commonly associated with the Viking period are the 'Olmütz' helmet, displayed in Vienna, and the 'St Wenceslas' helmet from the Treasury of Prague Cathedral. The dome of each is a one-piece forging. While there is no evidence that this technique was used by Norse armourers, the dating of these items and the diverse nature of the equipment used by the Vikings suggests helmets of this type may have been in use. Olaf the Saint is said to have deployed a unit of 100 picked men at the battle of Nesjar armed in coats of mail and 'foreign' helmets.

Armour

No complete hauberk of mail survives from the period and even fragments are rare. Mail retained its value as a form of defence until after the Middle Ages and would have been reused by succeeding generations. But this alone does not explain the paucity of finds. The level of usage among the Vikings may have been quite low. The poetry found within sagas, usually taken to be of much earlier date than the main body of text, frequently refers to byrnies. Mention of mail armour becomes more common when later events are described, perhaps implying more frequent use. The inference of Sturlusson's *Heimskringla* is that by the battle of Stamford Bridge (1066) the Norwegian army's lack of mail contributed to its defeat. The Norwegians had in fact left their armour aboard their ships at Riccall. The verses made up in the course of the battle by Harald Hardrada refer to the deficiency. The king himself had a mail-shirt considered important enough to have a name – 'Emma' – described as being unusually long at knee-length. Mail probably became more common and covered more of the body as the period progressed. The Continental fashion for mail coifs might also have been followed by the Vikings. The Huscarls of the late Saxon kingdom were, racially, of Danish origin. The Bayeux Tapestry indicates a similarity of gear between the Saxons and Normans, and the Normans certainly appear to be wearing coifs.

There exists a little evidence that lamellar armour was used in Scandinavia. Such armour is generally thought to be of Eastern origin. A few plates were found at Birka, now an isolated farm but once one of the major trading towns of central Sweden. The Eastern connections of this merchant settlement may explain the presence of this unusual find.

Front view of one of the 64 Gokstad shields (c. 900), nearly a metre (3.3 feet) in diameter. The curved metal strengthener on the back is visible. The shields on the Gokstad ship were originally painted either black or yellow, and bound round the rim in leather. (© Museum of Cultural History, University of Oslo, Norway)

There is also little evidence for the use of leather or fabric armour. Sturlusson, in the *Heimskringla*, mentions the gift of 13 body armours of reindeer hide to King Olaf the Saint. These were said to be more resistant to attack than mail hauberks. What may be quilted jacks of layered fabric armour appear on the Gotland tombstones. But this is uncertain because of the nature of this type of art.

Shields

The Gotland gravestones show warriors with what appear to be bucklers. The proportions of the figures that carry them suggest they were 24 inches (61 centimetres) or less in diameter. Such items may have been in use, but no archaeological evidence survives to confirm this. Had the sculptor of the Gotland gravestones attempted to depict a shield of 3 feet (0.9 metre) in diameter this would have produced a large blank expanse on the figure. The artist may have sacrificed strict proportions for the sake of producing a more detailed human subject. Other examples of this disregard for proportions so typical of the art of the period can be seen on the Gotland stones.

The largest group of surviving shields from the Viking Age was part of the ship burial at Gokstad. However, these shields may have been made specially for the burial and could be unrepresentative of those used in combat. Experiments carried out in 1990 by Daniel Ezra of City University revealed that a reproduction Gokstad shield was unwieldy in individual combat and tiring to use in close formation. Shield bosses have been relatively common finds. It has been assumed that many shields had metal rims; in fact, not a single excavated shield has been found with a complete metal rim. Organic components of shields are usually decayed to a point that defied early excavation techniques.

In the first centuries of the Viking period, shields appear to have always been circular. The curious oval shield that appears in the Oseberg tapestry has no parallel from archaeology. The kite-shaped shields, which were first beginning to appear in Scandinavia during the 11th century, were called *Holfinn-skjoldr*. The extent to which these were used in the late Viking Age is difficult to estimate, but Anglo-Norse Huscarls appear to have been almost exclusively equipped with them by the battle of Hastings. Such highly paid professional military retainers might be expected to have followed the latest Continental fashion.

Although shield blazons are often ascribed to Viking warriors in the much later Icelandic sagas, such evidence is of limited value. Such descriptions are usually thought to refer to medieval practices. Two characters in *Brennu-Njals Saga* are said to have had shields decorated with a dragon and a lion respectively. This may be anachronistic, but it is only necessary to consider the various animal representations on Bayeux Tapestry shields to recognize that they may have been in use less than a century earlier.

As mentioned in 'The Vikings in North America', symbolic shields were employed by Greenlanders in the Vinland expeditions, red to indicate warlike intentions and white for peace. The followers of Olaf the Saint are reputed to have carried white shields with a gilt, red or blue cross in 1015. This design was influenced by the aggressive Christianity of their leader but also served to distinguish them from their pagan opponents in battle.

WEAPONS

The typical offensive weapons found at Viking sites are the sword, axe, spear and bow. The majority of such sites are graves. Danish deposits of the early period include the same range of weapons as Swedish and Norwegian sites, but the early adoption of Christianity in Denmark brought an end to the custom of burying a warrior with his weapons, and this has reduced the sample of later Danish finds.

Swords

The commonest form of Viking sword (of which over 2,000 have been found in Scandinavia alone) is the long, straight, two-edged type. These were usually about 3 feet (0.9 metre) long with a simple cross-guard and some form of pommel. The blade was generally fullered for lightness and strength. The points of such swords were comparatively blunt as they were intended more for cutting than stabbing. Such weapons could be purely functional or highly decorative. Fittings of copper alloy were more common in Scandinavia than in the rest of Europe, but even so pommels and cross-guards of ferrous metal were the norm. When not in use the sword was carried in a scabbard of wood, usually covered in leather with a metal chape. The interior of the scabbard was ideally lined with sheepskin, the wool side inwards, the natural greases protecting the metal of the blade. Scabbards were usually suspended from a waist belt but could be worn over the shoulder on a baldric.

An important local variant of the longsword was the three-foot, single-edged version sometimes called the long-sax. This type is generally Norwegian in origin and has a single edge like the true sax commonly associated with the Saxons. Long-saxes are found with fittings that are roughly similar to those on swords. The majority of blades in this group appear to be made by pattern-welding techniques, which probably indicates they were high-status items.

Single-edged knives of more modest proportions are frequently found at Viking sites. Their enormous numbers (around 300 in the Coppergate dig of 1976–81 alone) argue for their use in everyday life as eating implements and tools. The somewhat larger saxes also encountered may have been hunting weapons rather than military arms. The level of decorative inlay on saxes of this type certainly points to their use by the wealthy.

Axes

Axes of the period are also decorated according to the owner's status. The splendid Mammen axe without its inlaid silver design would be no more than a common wood-chopping tool. The shape of axe-heads differed according to purpose, although it should be noted that a wood-axe might make a serviceable weapon. The broad-bladed axes wielded with two hands, which appear in the latter part of the period, are specialized items. By the time of Hastings they were almost the distinguishing mark of Anglo-Danish Huscarls and may have been a response to the increased use of mail. Axes with 'beards' or downward extensions to the blade have sometimes been identified as specifically Nordic. Given the widespread appearance of similar styles in the Middle Ages this is far from certain.

Staff weapons other than spears make no appearance in the Viking archaeological record. Perhaps funerary custom ignored the halberds and bills described in sagas or these are later intrusions into Old Norse literature. The curious mail-piercer described as part of Egil Skallagrimson's equipment at

Small axehead, 6.5 inches (16.5 centimetres) long, from Mammen, Jutland; it is inlaid with silver wire decoration in the 'Mammen style', to which it gave its name and which is characterized by writhing animal ornamentation. (Werner Forman Archive/National Museum, Copenhagen)

Brunanburh sounds like a glaive, a development of the agricultural bill-hook with additional prongs for use in combat. Such weapons are known from Merovingian Frankish graves and are often seen in illustrations post-dating the Vikings, but most examples are actually later medieval. The type does not seem to have been much used by Scandinavians of the 8th to the 11th centuries.

Spears

An early survey of Danish graves revealed that the spear was only the third most frequent weapon deposited after axe and sword. The value of the spear in fighting and hunting argues for a more widespread use than this evidence indicates. Since spearheads were cheaper and quicker to manufacture than the other favoured weapons of the period, it seems likely that spears were more usually carried than swords. The very cheapness of spears might account for their being used less often as grave goods.

Many of the spears associated with the Vikings are Carolingian imports identified by a characteristic broad blade and wings projecting from the socket. The latter feature is analogous to the cross-pieces on later boar-spears which prevent the shaft penetrating too deep into the victim. Modern experiment shows they could also be used to hook an opponent's shield aside. Spears with narrower blades may be interpreted as javelins, although a dual purpose is implied in literary sources. The intricate decoration sometimes found on this type of spear does not rule out their use as throwing weapons. The thrower might reasonably expect to recover his spear afterwards. Personalized decoration would allow instant recognition, and the thrower's skill would be undeniably shown when his weapon was extracted from a defeated foe.

MANUFACTURE OF WEAPONS

Accounts of Viking weapons manufacture, mostly contained in Icelandic sources, tend to concentrate on the more exalted heirlooms or even magical arms of heroes. The descriptions are often obscured by formulae of mystical significance. It is impossible to say how accurate these accounts might be, but a certain level of ceremony was probably expected in the creation of a special weapon. It may be that these curious descriptions of forging techniques are simply misunderstandings of the complexities of the smith's craft. The difficulties of attempting to use sagas as historical accounts are clearly demonstrated here.

Thidrik's Saga addresses itself to the forging of Mimming by the demi-god Volund the Smith. The unlikely-sounding process involves making a complete sword, filing it into dust and feeding it to domestic fowl so that it becomes thoroughly mixed with their droppings. This cycle is carried out twice before Volund is satisfied with the results. Independent evidence for the use of a similar technique by the *Rus* appears in Arabic manuscripts. These stories may simply be misunderstandings of the use of animal dung in forging techniques, possibly to introduce trace elements of nitrates into the blade.

The most desirable trace element in a ferrous metal weapon is carbon. Iron cannot be hardened until it contains at least 0.2 per cent carbon; at greater than I per cent carbon the compound is no longer steel. Viking smiths had to judge the amount of carbon by traditional methods handed down from previous masters. Barbarian smiths from the 2nd century BC onwards appear to have understood that the surface of iron could be carburized by exposure to carbon-based gases in a reducing atmosphere that excluded air. This could be achieved in a clay box containing carboniferous material at a high temperature.

Medium-quality steel for the forging of weapons could be produced by heating iron ore to 1200 degrees centigrade in a furnace alongside organic material such as bones. This could then be forged and drawn into rods with a steel surface. These could subsequently be twisted and forged with rods of lower carbon content into a composite blade giving a patterned appearance. This is the process sometimes called 'pattern-welding'.

Axes and spear-heads were normally made from plain steel, although weapons of both these types have been found constructed by pattern-welding techniques. Edges of harder steel were sometimes welded to less brittle weapon bodies formed from steel of a lower carbon content.

Evidence for all stages of the weapon-making process from the most basic levels can be seen at the Viking site at L'Anse aux Meadows in Newfoundland. The archaeologist Helge Ingstad found evidence for the working of bog-iron, a naturally occurring ferrous deposit on certain kinds of plant. The structure she identified as a smithy was at the extreme western limit of the known travels of the Vikings. This was part of a temporary settlement but was already capable of producing iron after what may have been only a few years' occupation.

The forging of the sword Ekkisax by the dwarf Alberich required the material of the blade to be buried in the ground for some time to improve its quality. This may refer to the method of burying bog-iron nodules to allow the non-ferrous inclusions to be absorbed out of the ore. After this period of curing, the remaining deposit could be worked into a thick bar at temperatures well below the melting point of iron. A lump of iron could be heated and squeezed to force out impurities in this way. Before modern metallurgical processes allowed the easy exploitation of haematite (an iron oxide ore), the majority of iron produced in Scandinavia was extracted in this way.

Although later than the Viking period, this 12th-century carving of a workshop scene shows an ard-stone, double bellows and a torch for the subdued lighting that allowed the smith to judge the state of the metal by radiant heat. This carving is from the west portico of Hylestad stave-church in Setesdal, Norway. (Werner Forman Archive/ Universitetets Oldsaksamling, Oslo)

Armour production

Our knowledge of the armour production in the Viking Age is obscured by the lack of relevant finds from archaeological sites. Organic body armour is unknown except in later literary references and in art that is difficult to interpret. The surviving shields are almost entirely grave deposits whose organic components have usually rotted away, and were excavated at a time when archaeological practice was less rigorous.

The principal form of metallic armour used by the Viking warrior was mail. There are numerous references in Old Norse literature to this type of defence. The only known form in north-western Europe appears as a series of interlocking rings either butted, fixed with a rivet or made as a complete circle.

Weaponsmith's workshop. This view of a Viking Age atelier illustrates most of the items needed by a smith for the production of arms and armour. (Gerry Embleton © Osprey Publishing Ltd)

The normal pattern of linking is four rings attached to each one. This can be increased or decreased to allow for variation in the shape of the wearer's body. Each ring is made from a circle of ferrous metal; the use of copper alloy rings as a decorative border can be dated back securely no earlier than the 14th century. The wire of which the rings are formed has to be drawn through a series of successively smaller holes in a metal plate to achieve the required thickness. Recent research suggests that iron rich in phosphorous displays superior properties for drawing in this manner.

Repairing weapons

The maintenance of weapons falls into two categories: specialist attention, either in the field or workshop, and improvised repairs to broken weapons. The latter might be as simple as straightening a bent sword-blade under one's

Matrix used in the manufacture of helmet plaques. The dancing figure wears a helmet whose horns terminate in birds' heads; his companion wears the mask of a wolf or bear. (Werner Forman Archive/Statens Historiska Museum, Stockholm)

foot. The Celts are described by classical authors as carrying this out in the midst of battle. The story is probably told as a comment on the poor workmanship of Celtic sword-blades and also appears in several Icelandic sagas in this context. The character Steinthor in *Eyrbyggja Saga* is mocked during one combat for the weakness of his sword-blade in a previous fight. Kjartan in *Laxdaela Saga* has a similar experience which actually leads to his death. *Kormak's Saga* tells how Kormak, a somewhat feckless young warrior, damages the edge of Skofnung (originally the sword of Hrolf Kraki, a king of Denmark) in combat. Attempting to re-sharpen the blade, he makes matters worse by enlarging the size of the notch. A proper re-sharpening was a skilled undertaking. *Droplaugarsona Saga* tells how a servant called Thorbjorn, known for his skill in the maintenance of weapons, was in the process of sharpening a sword for Helgi, one of the heroes of the saga. Grim, the brother of Helgi, later asks

for this weapon in particular. Personal whetstones, in one case fitted with a suspension ring and small enough to have been worn as an amulet, have been found in Viking contexts. Olaf Tryggvasson at the battle of Svöldr was so concerned to ensure his men had sharp swords that he began an issue of new weapons in the midst of the fight.

Swords could be carried and reused for generations, their significance and worth increasing as time passed. The value to the individual warrior was greater than that of a mere weapon. Ancient swords were status symbols and a nexus of power and influence. To the clan they could be a symbol of legitimacy intimately connected with luck and prosperity. Although the sagas speak of swords over 200 years old being used in combat, it can be assumed that great care would be taken of such items under normal circumstances.

Some ancient swords damaged beyond repair were re-forged into spearheads. Perhaps the best known of these was Grasida or 'Greyflank' which is mentioned in the story of Gisli Surson. The useful life of 'Greyflank' as a sword came to an end when it broke in a fight. The metal of the original sword may have been of sufficiently high quality to justify re-forging it. It is possible that the fragments were thought to be charged with the virtue of the ancient blade. There was malign intent in the act of re-forging: a sorcerer was specifically chosen for the task. An unusually short handle only eight inches (20 centimetres) long was provided for 'Greyflank' as a spear, a feature which may reflect some unknown ceremonial meaning. The pattern-welded weapon was then used in the murders of Vestein and Thorgrim.

The Viking Longship

EVOLUTION OF THE VIKING LONGSHIP

There are few more potent symbols of an era than the Viking longship. To the Vikings themselves, it was the ultimate expression of their dynamic culture, its importance reflected in the profusion of ship representations found on their memorial stones, coinage and in their graffiti. Love of their ships also continued into the afterlife, as evidenced in the magnificent Gokstad and Oseberg ship burials and in their custom of using a man's ship as his funeral pyre. Their pride in these elegant vessels is equally apparent in the great Icelandic sagas where we find names bestowed upon them such as *Oarsteed*, *Surf Dragon*, *Fjord Elk*, *Ocean-Striding Bison* and *Great Serpent*.

The demands of warfare, trade and exploration led to distinct variations in the basic design of these ships, each kind being distinguished by its own technical name. Small boats were categorized by the number of oars they employed; for example, a six-oared boat was known as a *sexaeringr*, and general-purpose ships of 12 to 32 oars, such as the Gokstad ship, were known as *karvi*. Longships, like those found at Ladby and Skuldelev, with a minimum of 20 rowing positions, were named *snekkja*, which translates as 'thin and projecting', and larger warships, like the Skuldelev 2 and Roskilde 6 longships, were known as *skei*, meaning 'that which cuts through the water'. Giant warships from the latter part of the Viking Age are well documented in the sagas and are called *drekar* or dragons, no doubt in recognition of their fearsomely carved prows. The generic term for all of these warships is *langskip* or longship. Cargo-carrying vessels were known as *knarrs* or *kaupskips*, meaning 'trade ships'. It should be pointed out, however, that contemporary sources sometimes use these terms in a somewhat confusing manner, making it occasionally difficult to place some surviving ship remains into a suitable category.

In a land criss-crossed by fjords, lakes and rivers, the significance of seaworthy vessels quickly becomes clear. As we shall see, this seafaring culture would develop a line of vessels that would evolve through the Stone Age, Bronze Age and Migration Age, finding their purest expression in the magnificent ships built between the 9th and 13th centuries.

The Gokstad ship as reconstructed, in the Viking Ship Museum at Oslo. (© Museum of Cultural History, University of Oslo, Norway, photographer Eirik Irgens Johnsen)

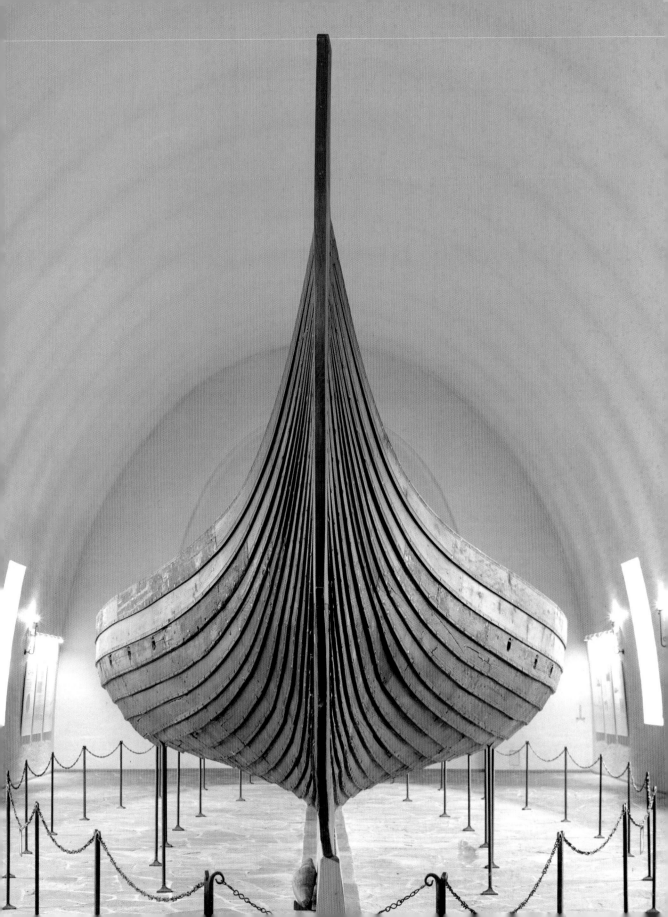

EARLY SKIN AND LOG BOATS

Some time at the close of the Ice Age, between 8000 and 6000 BC, bands of nomadic hunter-fishers roaming ever northwards in the wake of the retreating ice began to settle along Norway's north-western coast.

Hunting the big game of the arctic and exploiting the abundance of marine life in the off-shore fishing grounds, they used the sea as their highway, and from the very beginning, seaworthy boats were a necessity. Experts generally agree that the craft in which they braved these icy seas were similar in form to the arctic

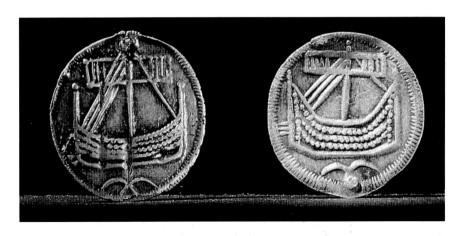

These 9th-century silver coins depict Viking ships. They were found in the Viking marketplace at Birka, Sweden. (Werner Forman Archive / Statens Historiska Museet, Stockholm)

umiak. In a design that has remained unchanged to this day, the *umiak* is constructed by stretching and sewing overlapping waterproofed seal skins over a wooden framework of ribs and longitudinal stringers. The cultural importance of such boats to these people is reflected in the numerous depictions of them in prehistoric rock art. The most famous examples can be found at Evenhus, near Trondheim, where a collection of carvings, boldly incised into a rock face, depict a very specific type of craft. Deep sided and tub-like in appearance, these boats certainly bear a striking resemblance to the *umiak*. The ends of their hulls rise sharply, one end usually terminating in a kind of lip, the other – which is generally higher – often ending in two short, curved parallel lines. These two lines, which probably depict the prow, have been interpreted as handles, a feature of the *umiak* that is essential when beaching such a delicate craft. Some of the boats also have vertical or horizontal lines carved inside their hulls, possibly an attempt to depict the aforementioned wooden framework.

Meanwhile, in the more temperate climes of southern Scandinavia, men were also venturing out on to the water. While no doubt aware of the skin boat, these inland tribes, taking advantage of the vast areas of forests, began constructing log boats of gradually increasing sophistication. These ranged from small, simple dugouts perhaps 4 metres (13 feet) long with a narrow beam of less than 1 metre (3.3 feet), to much longer examples which may have been stabilized by outriggers and given a higher gunwale by attaching additional pieces of wood to the sides. These boats, while perfectly adequate for fishing and limited travel on calm, inland waterways, would have been quite unsuitable for any kind of ocean-going activity. They did, however, give rise to a wood-based boatbuilding tradition that absorbed the technology of the skin boat, and, by the Bronze Age, had begun to produce Scandinavia's first plank-built vessels.

The Hjortspring boat

For the northern world, the coming of the Bronze Age heralded an era of thriving trade and expansion, and it was the lure of wealth that would be the catalyst in the next stage of Scandinavian marine development.

With the introduction of metal into northern Europe near the end of the third millennium BC, shipbuilding techniques began to evolve as never before. Over the centuries, the search for copper and tin, necessary for the production of bronze weapons and tools, led to ever expanding areas of trade and broadened Scandinavian seafaring experience. This in turn led to increasing refinements of design which, by 1500 BC, saw these people voyaging far beyond their native waters and, while staying in sight of land, making regular trading expeditions to Britain, Ireland and possibly even to France, Spain and the Mediterranean.

Once again, the importance this society placed on its ships has left us with thousands of rock carvings in Norway, Denmark and Sweden, which form a unique archive of these Bronze Age craft. They depict flotillas of broad-beamed, open boats, with keels and gunwales that project like beaks fore and aft, well beyond the hull. Some of the craft are small and plain, while others, elaborately detailed, feature prows terminating in animal heads and stylized depictions of the crew, who are either paddling the craft or, in some instances, brandishing weapons.

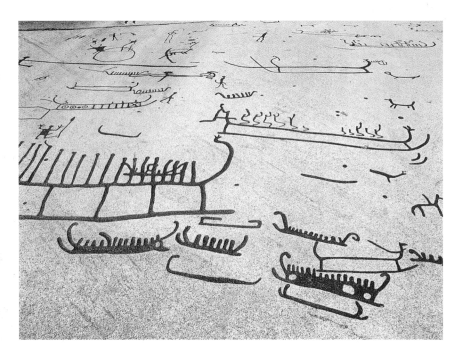

This Bronze Age rock carving from Vitlycke, Sweden, depicts a fleet of vessels. Many of these carvings feature vertical lines rising from the hull, which may represent the crew or perhaps the number of paddles deployed. (Werner Forman Archive)

In 1921, the reality behind these carvings came to light when such a vessel was excavated from the Hjortspring bog on the island of Åls in southern Denmark. Presumably seized as a trophy of war, it is the earliest plank-built boat yet discovered in Scandinavia, and around 350 BC, had been filled with the captured weapons and equipment of a defeated enemy and sunk in the bog as a votive offering. Though the Hjortspring boat can actually be dated to the early Iron Age, its resemblance to the vessels depicted in rock carvings from the Bronze Age is obvious. Just over 18 metres (59 feet) long and 2 metres (6.6 feet) wide amidships, the hull consists of only seven pieces of lime-wood sewn together with gut and caulked with resin. The boat would appear to be a large war canoe and was equipped with a steering oar at each end and paddles for 20 men. The bottom is formed from a single broad plank, which is dished out and fashioned in a gentle curve running fore and aft. As this plank becomes narrower at each end, the hollowing-out becomes more acute; here separate end pieces, similarly hollowed-out, are sewn on to the bottom plank and form the prow and stern. It is from the boat's bottom plank and these pre-cut end pieces that the curious beak-like projections extend, forming the double prow and stern that characterize these vessels. Completing the hull are two broad, overlapping planks on each side that are sewn to the bottom and form a garboard and sheerstrake. These planks do not meet where they converge at the bow and stern, but instead are run into the hollowed-out end pieces.

The inner supports consist of slender hazel branches that are curved like ribs from gunwale to gunwale, spaced 1 metre (3.3 feet) apart and lashed to the hull by means of cleats left proud when the planks were formed. This unique method of construction, which gives a remarkable degree of flexibility to the

A small-scale reconstruction of the Hjortspring boat, 350 BC. A full-scale replica, the Tilia, was tested out by an experienced crew employing 18 paddles. The boat proved fast, manoeuvrable and seaworthy, and in sheltered waters, it averaged a respectable 6 knots. (Natural History Museum of Denmark)

overall structure of the vessel, would continue well into the 10th century. Spanning these ribs are thwarts for the crew, which are angled in such a way as to maximize the power of a downward paddle thrust. The double row of props supporting them further strengthens the thinly planked hull.

From an evolutionary point of view, the Hjortspring boat is an almost perfect amalgam of the principal elements of both skin and log boat construction and embodies the strength, lightness and flexibility that would become the hallmarks of Scandinavian shipbuilding. That these virtues had been consolidated and improved upon over the next 700 years would become evident when an ocean-going vessel from the dawn of the Migration Age was discovered at Nydam in south Jutland in 1863.

The Nydam ship

Like the Hjortspring boat, the largest vessel found at Nydam was undoubtedly a warship and had been filled with military equipment before being sunk as a sacrificial offering around AD 350–400. The ship is a massive, clinker-built, open rowing-boat measuring about 23.5 metres (77 feet) long, 3.5 metres (11.5 feet) wide and 1.2 metres (3.9 feet) deep. Built entirely of oak, its spine consists of a bottom plank to which are fixed raked stem and stern pieces. The hull is completed by ten strakes, which are attached five to each side of the bottom plank, the sheerstrake being reinforced by a scarfed gunwale. All ten strakes are fixed to the stem and stern, which are rebated to receive them. Running the full length of the hull, each strake, measuring over 20 metres (66 feet) long and 50 centimetres (19.7 inches) wide, is formed from a single piece of timber. While primitive in concept, the mere production of such a colossal, flexible plank testifies to the skill of these Iron Age shipwrights. Unlike the Hjortspring boat, these overlapping, or 'clinker-built' strakes are not sewn together, but are riveted with iron nails clenched over small, square roves on the inside of the hull, the first example of a tradition that persisted through the Viking Age to our own day.

The ship's substantial ribs are hewn from suitably formed timbers and are lashed to the hull via cleats left standing proud on the planking. Fifteen thwarts, spaced 1 metre (3.3 feet) apart and supported by a series of props, would have accommodated the oarsmen and completed the skeleton. The vessel was propelled by 30 oars, and a similar number of barb-shaped rowlocks were lashed to the gunwales. The ship was steered by a large, paddle-shaped rudder, which was found near the stern. No trace of any fixture for a mast was found, and it is unlikely that so narrow and steep-sided a vessel could have been sailed with any degree of confidence. That does not mean to say that the

The reconstructed 4th-century Nydam ship. In an attempt to counteract the inherent weakness of the bottom plank, the ship has been given a rather narrow profile and sharp bows. Note the archaic rudder and the rowlocks lashed to the gunwale. (Archäologisches Landesmuseum, Schleswig, Germany)

vessel was unseaworthy, for it was in such ships as those found at Nydam and at Sutton Hoo in East Anglia that Saxon warriors crossed the North Sea to raid and later colonize England. We can be sure, however, that some of these voyages in such shallow open vessels, which had no keel and could be prone to hogging or swamping, ended in disaster.

Nevertheless, the advances made in the Nydam ship are obvious: a fixed steerboard and oars replacing paddles provides a more efficient method of steering and propulsion, and iron-riveted planking ensures a more robust and secure hull. What is still lacking, however, is the strength and stability that would be achieved by the introduction of a keel.

That this problem was at least partially overcome by the beginning of the 8th century is apparent in the Kvalsund ship excavated at Sunmøre in western Norway.

The Kvalsund ship

Built around AD 700, the Kvalsund ship is a large, open, sea-going vessel 18 metres (59 feet) long, 3 metres (9.8 feet) wide and 80 centimetres (31.5 inches) deep. Like the two previous craft described, it was deposited in a bog as a votive offering, and is the first vessel found in Scandinavia that utilizes a keel.

Although the ship's backbone still consists of a bottom plank, it is fashioned in such a way as to create a thick integral runner along its external length, and a rudimentary keel has been formed. Although far from perfect, the arrangement is a major step forward, strengthening the bottom of the ship against hogging and facilitating the shaping of a graceful, broader and more spacious hull. More importantly, the stability achieved presents the option of mounting a sail, for the provision of a keel also allows a vessel to partially heel over when under sail without capsizing. Although no mast or rigging was discovered, everything about this ship's construction points to an ocean-going vessel that could be sailed or rowed.

The clinker-built hull is constructed entirely of oak and is fixed with iron rivets. Now, however, the strakes have become narrower, there are more of them and each strake is fashioned from several lengths of timber. This gives an even greater degree of flexibility to the hull and cuts out the arduous task of locating and preparing the enormous lengths of timber previously required. The ship's ribs are of pine and are lashed to the hull, but in this case not to the bottom or keel-plank, thus allowing the flexible hull to 'work' independently of the keel in heavy seas. Ten rowlocks are fixed to each gunwale by wooden pegs, known as trenails, and 11 evenly spaced thwarts, or crossbeams, 1 metre (3.3 feet) apart, brace the structure and double as benches for the oarsmen. The two high, curving stem and stern pieces are lightly decorated and are fixed to the keel-plank by flat joints.

In addition, the Kvalsund ship is the first example of what was to become the classic method of mounting a fixed rudder to the right side of the hull aft, the 'steerboard' or starboard side (from the Old Norse *styri*, to steer). A cone-shaped boss is nailed to the hull, and a withy passed through the rudder is threaded through holes drilled in the boss and hull, and made fast inboard to a triangular-shaped rudder rib, which is strengthened on the starboard side. The rudder rib and a matching forward bulkhead are not lashed, but nailed to the hull, their sides carved in a series of steps to accommodate the ship's overlapping strakes. The neck of the rudder is secured to the gunwale by means of an adjustable strap, and a tiller facilitates steering. This arrangement, while securing the rudder in an efficient manner, still allows it the flexibility to turn on its own longitudinal axis.

Almost every element of the Kvalsund ship's construction places it firmly at the beginning of a new era of Scandinavian shipbuilding technology, which would come to its full flowering in the 9th and 10th centuries.

The sail

Perhaps the most enduring mystery in this process of evolution is why it took such a resourceful, seafaring people until the 8th century to adopt the sail. The first evidence for its introduction in Scandinavia comes in the form of ship depictions on early 8th-century picture stones from the island of Gotland in Sweden, but being such energetic traders, it is difficult to believe that the Scandinavians were unaware of its existence before then. By that time the sail had been widely used in the Mediterranean for centuries and must also have been a familiar sight in parts of western Europe where Roman influence had prevailed (although that influence never actually extended into Scandinavia).

One reason for this apparent lack of enterprise may be that prior to the 8th century, while overseas voyaging was not uncommon, most marine activity actually took place in Scandinavia's coastal waters, where oar power was an adequate means of propulsion. In other words, the sail was not a prerequisite for water-borne travel.

Also, until the emergence of the Kvalsund ship, the lack of a keel and reliance on a bottom plank had effectively constrained ship design, producing narrow, sharp-sided vessels that did not readily lend themselves to the stress and strain imposed by mast and sail.

The truth is, there is no satisfactory answer to the question, but once the sail was – quite literally – taken on board, its use brought about a number of significant changes in the way that ships would be constructed in the Viking Age.

This model of the Kvalsund ship shows to perfection its sleek lines that clearly anticipate the magnificent vessels of the Viking Age. Note the classic arrangement of the 'steerboard' and the low-slung, roomy hull. (Bergens Sjørfartsmuseum, Norway)

THE VIKING AGE

With the introduction of a true keel, sturdy and T-shaped in cross section, the bottom of the ship began to expand in a series of gently sloping, clinker-built strakes. Below the waterline the ribs were still lashed to the strakes via cleats but, as we have seen, not to the first strake, or garboard, and keel. Where the bottom strakes met the waterline, what had previously been a reinforced gunwale was now transformed into a significantly thicker strake known as a *meginhúfr* (Old Norse: 'strong plank'). This strake, which along with the keel provided longitudinal strength to the ship, also substantially reinforced the hull where it met the waterline and facilitated the transition from bottom to sides. Attached to it were crossbeams, which spanned the tops of the ribs and were fixed to them with trenails. In order to avoid the ship being swamped while heeling over when under sail, the ship's sides were heightened by the addition of a number of strakes. As the upper strakes also had to withstand buffeting from waves and endure the strain exerted on the hull while heeling over, they were nailed to L-shaped knees, which in turn were attached to each end of the crossbeams. Further support was provided by a series of top ribs, one for every other knee.

A Norse ship with dragon-head prow incised on a piece of wood. (Werner Forman Archive/Maritime Museum, Bergen)

The higher gunwales made the use of rowlocks impractical, so now oar holes were pierced at an appropriate height in one of the upper strakes, which was generally made thicker in order to absorb the wear and tear generated by rowing. The crossbeams that previously served as benches for the oarsmen were now redundant for that purpose and were rebated to receive a deck of carefully fitted planking that was generally left loose, allowing access to the hull for baling, repairs and storage.

Support for the mast began immediately above the keel in the shape of a massive block of timber known as the *kjerringa* (Old Norse: 'the crone') or keelson. Resting over the keel but not actually attached to it, the keelson might span up to four ribs, to which it was fixed with trenails. Fitted with a socket to take the mast, its primary function was to evenly spread the weight of the mast and the strain exerted by it when the ship was under sail. Immediately in front of the socket, the keelson sprouted a vertical arm that supported the mast until it reached deck level. Here, the mast was braced by another large block of timber that was slotted fork-like to accommodate it. Known as a 'mast-partner' or 'mast-fish' from its fish-tailed shape, this humpbacked member straddled four or six crossbeams into which it was rebated and fixed with trenails. Additional support on each side was provided by knees, nailed to it and the crossbeams. The mast was further secured by shrouds and fore and back stays. A large, deep rudder was attached to the starboard side aft, as described on the Kvalsund ship.

It is important to remember that these innovations, which took place over 150 years and culminated in such magnificent vessels as those found at Gokstad and Oseberg, were only made possible by the consummate skill of the Viking shipwright.

SHIPWRIGHTS AND SHIPBUILDING

In 1893, when the Gokstad replica *Viking* was being built, it proved impossible to find in Norway an oak tree of suitable dimensions from which to fashion the 18 metre (59 feet) keel, and eventually, an appropriate length of wood had to be imported from Canada.

Incredible though this may seem in a country renowned for its supplies of timber, the reason for this scarcity of oak becomes apparent in light of the following. The archaeologist Ole Crumlin-Pedersen has calculated that 50–58 cubic metres (1766–2048 cubic feet) of oak would have been required to build a longship of between 20 and 25 metres (66 and 82 feet) in length. If each tree used was 1 metre (3.3 feet) in diameter and about 5 metres (16.4 feet) high, this would involve felling 11 such trees and one additional tree, measuring 15–18 metres (49–59 feet) high, for the keel.

Even allowing for exaggeration, the size of fleets mentioned in the sagas and other contemporary documents suggests that thousands of such ships were built

in the Viking Age, and there is little doubt that Norway's shortage of oak at the end of the 19th century was, in part at least, a direct legacy of that initial widescale plundering of resources a thousand years earlier. Naturally, other woods were also used, including pine, ash, lime, willow and birch, sometimes for their particular qualities, or when oak was unavailable.

A master shipwright would have had a team of artisans working under him, all of whom would be skilled in one task or another. One of the most important of these tasks was the ability to identify in the forest those trees that would lend themselves to the shaping of various parts of the ship's structure. Tall forest oaks would provide timber for a keel and planking, while masts, yards, spars and oars would be cut from pine. Isolated field oaks with low curving boughs would be valuable for ribs, stem and stern pieces, and a mast-fish or rudder could be formed from the thick trunk. Where possible, a carpenter would also take advantage of the strength of a natural joint where a branch grew out from a trunk, as when fashioning a keelson with a vertical

The flagship Mora, *in which William, Duke of Normandy, led the Norman invasion fleet across the Channel in 1066. Oars are being deployed to manoeuvre the ship, and while the crew make ready to sail, a man in the bow fixes the* Mora's *dragon-head to her prow. We are told that William gave the signal to set sail by lighting a lantern hung at the* Mora's *mast-head and by the sounding of a horn. At the stern, a squire displays William's colours and sounds a blast-horn. Provisions, equipment and weapons are being ferried to the larger ships by small cargo boats, while* knarrs *and cargo vessels, which are generally shieldless, are used to transport the horses. (Steve Noon © Osprey Publishing Ltd)*

supporting arm. Smaller, naturally angled pieces of timber were worked into knees of varying size and into rowlocks for smaller craft.

The task of locating such trees was generally undertaken in the early winter when they were easier to identify and the lack of undergrowth made the transportation of timber to the shipyard less arduous. Also, freshly cut timber is generally more stable in cold weather and is less likely to dry out and crack before it is used. Trees would be carefully felled using axes and wedges and, when appropriate, would be cleaned and split on site. No doubt on occasion, the master shipwright himself would supervise the felling of a particular tree from which would be fashioned the keel or other parts that were critical in the ship's construction.

Planks were formed by splitting logs radially, using axes, chisels and wooden or metal wedges. First, the logs were split in half, then quartered, then split into eighths and so on until a trunk 1 metre (3.3 feet) in diameter produced around 20 planks. The saw was never used in this process, for by splitting logs this way and following the grain instead of cutting across it, the carpenter did not compromise the strength of the timber. He was then able to produce thin, incredibly flexible planking that, if used while still green, could be curved and twisted when forming the hull. As we will see, the bottom planking on the Gokstad ship was only 2.6 centimetres (1 inch) thick.

Very few parts of the felled tree would be discarded. Wood was also required for trenails, rigging blocks, stringers, rakkes, clamps and the stocks on which the ship was built. Bast fibres, found just below the bark, were twisted into rope,

while sawdust and chippings were used for firewood and to smoke fish, cheese and meat. In addition, partly finished timbers that could be used at a later date have been found in bogs where they had been stored to keep them moist.

Close examination of the wood used in Viking ships indicates that the axe was by far the most important of the shipwright's tools. This is also evident in the shipbuilding scenes depicted in the Bayeux Tapestry where no fewer than four different types of axe are being used to fell trees, lop branches and fashion and finish planking. Also in use were the adze, gouge, plane, hammer, chisel, auger, various moulding irons and the knife. There is, however, little evidence of the saw, though it must have been used on occasion. Working closely with the shipwright was the blacksmith, who would maintain these tools, forge new ones and produce the thousands of nails and roves used in a ship's construction.

A shipwright did not rely on plans to build his ship, but worked instead within a tradition passed down through successive generations, where an experienced eye and rule of thumb dictated the vessel's final shape and size. Whether the commission was for a warship, *knarr* or coastal trader, each ship shared the same basic characteristics, and by not straying too far from acceptable

The Skuldelev 2 replica 'Havhingsten fra Glendalough' *under construction at Roskilde in 2003. (Keith Durham)*

ratios of length, breadth and depth, the shipwright could incorporate specific demands or regional variations into his design.

In the tradition of the Hjortspring, Nydam and Kvalsund vessels, ships of the Viking Age were built using the 'shell first' method of construction, internal reinforcements only being installed when the bottom strakes reached the waterline. Construction began by preparing the T-shaped keel, laying it on secure, level stocks and using heavy rocks to jam it in an upright position. Fore and aft stems were then scarfed to the keel and the whole structure firmly supported at each end by a pair of tall wooden props. This initial stage would have always been closely supervised by the shipwright, as a poorly shaped keel or badly scarfed stems could not only have far-reaching consequences for the ship's handling qualities, but could also result in the subsequent misalignment of other elements in the vessel's structure. Once the keel was laid and the ship's spine completed, the shaping of the hull could begin.

Each individual strake was made up of a number of scarfed pieces, every overlapping joint being secured by three nails clenched inboard over small iron roves. Traditionally, the external open end of these joints would always face

Ship construction, 9th century

Interior of the Oseberg ship (**1**), showing the method of attaching the strakes to the ribs by means of integral cleats. Note the L-shaped *meginhúfr*, third strake from the gunwale. (**2**) shows the mast support system of the Gokstad ship. Note the arched mast-fish and the integral, vertical arm rising from the keelson, which braces the mast. Also shown are the upper ribs, shield rack and the shuttered oar holes. (**3**) shows the method of attaching the steerboard to the hull. Note the strong plank that forms the vertical rudder rib through which the rudder withy is secured. Weather vanes from ships' prows and mastheads (**4**) often ended their days on church steeples, such as this one from Söderala, Sweden.

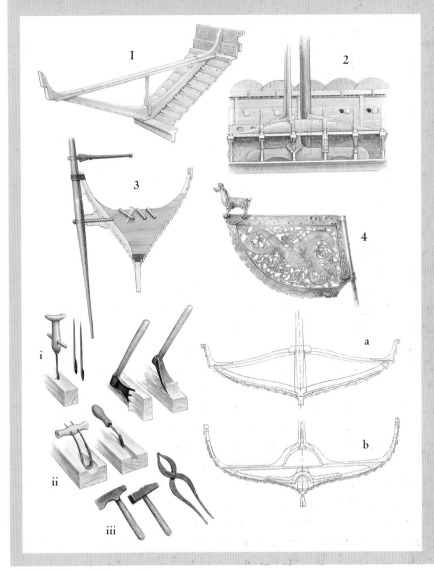

Various tools used in shipbuilding:
i   top row – from the left – a breast-auger and bits, side-axe, adze.
ii middle row – two moulding irons.
iii bottom row – from the left – a hafted wedge, hammer and tongs.

Cross sections of the Oseberg ship (**a**) and the Gokstad ship (**b**). The higher freeboard and more robust nature of the Gokstad ship is clearly apparent. (Steve Noon © Osprey Publishing Ltd)

aft in order to minimize any ingress of water. When building up the hull, it was also important to ensure that such joints were staggered and not placed one above the other, where they could create a potential weakness. If this was allowed to happen, the ship was said to be 'pieced'.

The strakes were not cut straight edged but were shaped in relation to their position in the hull, and were trimmed using a side-axe. The upper external edge, the 'land', was planed back in order to form a smooth, angled surface and ensured a flush fit where the next strake overlapped. Just above the lower internal edge, a groove was incised using a moulding iron, and into it was stuffed a twisted rope of animal hair, generously caulked in pine tar, making the joint as waterproof as possible.

Having shaped the first, or garboard strake, it would then be bored and nailed to the underside of the projecting ridge at the top of the keel. This joint could be prone to leaking and consequently was well packed with rope and tar. The second strake was then caulked and clamped to the garboard, and where they overlapped, holes were bored at approximately 18-centimetre (7-inch) intervals and the two strakes were secured together with iron nails. A third strake was attached to the second in a similar manner, then riveted, and so on, until the hull was complete. As each subsequent strake was added and the shape of the hull began to emerge, the shipwright could determine its symmetry at the clamping stage by varying the angle or width of each strake in relation to its neighbour.

While this would be achieved largely by means of a practised hand and experienced eye, some experts feel that at this stage the shipwright may have availed himself of a boat ell. This was a long stick marked with pre-recorded measurements, which allowed him to check the position of each strake at various points along its length against a series of knots in a fixed line running from stem to stern. As an alternative, templates may have been used, or some kind of boat level to measure the angle of the strakes. It should be stressed, however, that many shipwrights, including some traditional boatbuilders in Scandinavia today, would shun the use of such aids.

Once the *meginhúfr* had been attached at the waterline, the keelson, ribs, crossbeams and vertical knees would be fitted. Four to six strakes per side would be added above the *meginhúfr*, oar holes pierced and the upper ribs attached. The mast-fish would be fixed to the crossbeams and a rudder fashioned and secured starboard aft. The ship would be given numerous coatings of pine tar and then launched. She would be checked for leaks, and ballast would be added and adjusted until the shipwright was happy with the way the vessel sat in the water. The ship was then ready for fitting out.

The mast was stepped and a yard secured to it by means of a rakke. If the vessel was a trader, two to four oars would be fashioned, but if it was a warship this could involve producing between 30 and 60 oars of varying lengths. Decking would be laid, cleats fitted, then, depending on how affluent the prospective owner felt, the ship could be furnished with a gangplank, balers, water barrels and an iron anchor, which would be forged by the blacksmith and no doubt constituted a major expense in itself.

Working in close proximity to the shipyard would be craftsmen and women who would produce sails and a variety of ropes used in the ship's rigging. The archaeological and documentary evidence for sails and rigging from the Viking Age is minimal, but close examination of ship representations on picture stones and coins from the 8th to the 11th centuries gives us some useful clues; so too does the study of ethnological material from northern Norway, where up to the middle of the 20th century, traditional fishing boats still relied on large,

A reconstruction of the 11th-century Viking trading ship Roar Ege. *Beautifully constructed, her hull terminates in a steeply rising prow and stern, giving this fine little ship a rakish appearance. (The Viking Ship Museum, Roskilde)*

rectangular sails for propulsion. Weaving and sewing the cloth for sails that ranged in size from 45 to 100 square metres (484 to 1076 square feet) must have been an enormous undertaking, employing large numbers of men and women and, as a consequence, must have been an extremely costly, though essential, accessory. As far as we know, sails were generally woven from coarse wool, were sometimes of double thickness and were waxed or oiled to proof them against the elements. In order to stop them sagging and losing their shape when they did become sodden, they may have been reinforced by a diagonal latticework of rope, or thin leather strips. It is possible that many of the ships portrayed on the 9th-century Gotland picture stones depict just such an arrangement, which would certainly create the distinctive diamond patterns so often displayed on their sails.

Most of these depictions also show a web-like arrangement of what appears to be reefing lines running from the lower edge of the sail. These may well have functioned in a similar fashion to lines used on northern Norwegian fishing boats, which were loosely woven through the sail cloth and when tightened would bunch up the areas between them, thereby reducing the area of sail. Alternatively, three or four horizontal rows of reefing lines may have been employed, allowing the sail to be rolled up, tied and effectively shortened. The edges of the sail would invariably have been strengthened with a border of rope, which would also have acted as a point of purchase for the priares, sheets, bowline and tackline.

Ropes were fashioned from horsetails, bast, hemp and the skin of the walrus, whale and seal. From the existing evidence, standing rigging was both simple and minimal. Picture stones, coins and graffiti invariably depict vessels with two or three shrouds supporting the mast. These were apparently secured by means of cleats on the upper strakes, or via holes bored through the ribs or through iron osier rings attached to ribs or beams. Additional support for the mast was provided by fore and back stays secured near the prow and stern. Running rigging no doubt included a halyard, which, passing through a hole near the top of the mast, facilitated the hoisting and lowering of the yard and sail. The angle of the yard would have been determined by two braces, while sheets, tacklines, priares and a bowline would have given ample control of the sail. Cordage was manoeuvred by a variety of blocks, rope-cleats, beckets, shackles and shroud pins, some of which have survived in the Oseberg and Gokstad burials. Ideas of how they functioned, however, can only be speculative.

KARVI

By the beginning of the 9th century, advances in ship design and the experience gained under sail by two generations of Norse seafarers led to the first Viking attacks on the coasts of Europe. These raids were doubtless carried out by crews who would carry trade goods with which to barter, but if an opportunity presented itself, would take by force of arms what they desired. It is almost certain that the ships they employed were *karvi*. Equally at home as a raider, trader or coastal pleasure craft, well-preserved examples of such vessels were discovered in royal burial mounds at Oseberg and Gokstad in Norway.

The Oseberg ship

The Oseberg ship, without doubt the most spectacular vessel to have survived from the Viking Age, was excavated throughout the summer of 1904 on a site near the Oseberg farm on the western side of Oslo Fjord in the county of Vestfold, Norway.

The ship had been buried not from far from the sea, on a flat piece of land close to a stream. It had originally been covered by an impressive grave mound measuring 6.5 metres (21.3 feet) high and over 40 metres (131 feet) in diameter, but when Professor Gabriel Gustafson began his excavation, centuries of subsidence had reduced the height of the mound to a mere 2.5 metres (8.2 feet). As the mound had settled, the resulting compression formed

The beautifully restored Oseberg ship as she is today in the Viking Ship Museum, Bygdøy, Oslo. The coiling prow, lavishly decorated with a filigree of intertwined creatures, terminates in a staring serpent's head. Thought to be the final resting place of Queen Åsa, the Oseberg ship bears mute testimony to the consummate skills of the Viking craftsmen who built her.
(© Museum of Cultural History, University of Oslo, Norway)

a virtually airtight seal over the grave, and this factor, combined with the unique preservative qualities of the damp blue clay in which the ship rested, kept decay to a minimum and helped preserve not only the ship, but almost all of the ancillary equipment buried with it.

The grave had not, however, lain undisturbed. In the early Middle Ages, grave robbers had made a tunnel into the mound, hacked their way through the prow of the ship and broken through the roof of the burial chamber. The skeletons of the two occupants, both women, along with some of their belongings, had been scattered; not surprisingly, archaeologists found no trace of jewellery or precious metals left in the grave.

By carrying out dendroanalysis on the oak logs used to construct the burial chamber, it has been possible to date the interment to the year AD 834. The ship, however, had been built many years before, the decoration on its prow and stern dating it to around the year AD 800. Smaller than a regular longship, it falls into the *karvi* class of vessels and, as we shall see, was designed as a high-born person's pleasure craft.

Except where noted, the ship is constructed entirely of oak, and is 21.58 metres (70.8 feet) long and 5.1 metres (16.7 feet) wide at its broadest point amidships. It is a very shallow vessel, the height from the base of the keel amidships to the gunwale being a mere 1.58 metres (5.2 feet). The keel is T-shaped in cross section, is 19.8 metres (65 feet) long and is made from two pieces of timber. These are joined about 4 metres (13 feet) from the stern by means of a scarf joint secured by iron rivets. Amidships, the keel is 25 centimetres (9.8 inches) deep and 20 centimetres (7.9 inches) wide, tapering to 13 centimetres (5.1 inches) towards the prow and stern. The base of the keel is formed in a long, shallow curve running fore to aft, placing the greatest draught amidships where the hull is broadest and making the ship very easy to turn. The magnificently carved prow and stern are cut from carefully chosen pieces of oak and are secured by scarf joints where they join the main keel timber.

The hull is made up of 12 overlapping strakes, nine of which form the bottom of the ship. A tenth, the *meginhúfr*, facilitates the transition from bottom to side, the 11th and 12th being the only two strakes above the waterline. Where the strakes overlap, they are caulked with tarred wool and riveted together using round-headed, iron nails clenched over small square roves in the usual clinker-built way. The individual strakes are at their thickest amidships and tend to taper towards the bow and stern. The nine strakes below the waterline, which need to be thin and flexible, are trimmed to a thickness of 2 centimetres (0.8 inches), whereas the 11th and 12th, which need to be stronger, are between 2.5 and 3 centimetres (0.98 and 1.2 inches) thick. As usual, the *meginhúfr*, given its strengthening role, is of a much heavier construction. Resembling an inverted L, it juts out like a cornice at the waterline, allowing the gently angled strakes below to meet the two upper strakes that rise up almost at a right angle from it. It is this feature that gives the ship its low-slung, rakish lines, but such low sides would also have made it extremely prone to swamping in rough seas.

All joints in the strakes are scarfed, though not all of them have the exposed edge of the joint facing aft as they should. In addition, some 'piecing' is evident around the bow and stern, but internal reinforcements at these points are sound enough to withstand any potential weakness to the hull.

The garboard strake is nailed to the keel, and strakes two to eight are lashed with whalebristle to the ship's 17 evenly spaced ribs by means of corresponding rows of pierced cleats, which stand proud along the inside face of the strakes. Trimmed smooth on their upper sides, the ribs have a ridge on their lower edge, which is pierced to accommodate the whalebristle lashings running from the strake-cleats. The ninth strake and the *meginhúfr* are riveted to the upper section

The Oseberg ship. The ship was found in a trench with its rudder in place and its prow pointing south toward the open sea. It contained the skeletons of two women. The ship was secured in the grave by means of a stout hawser tied to a large stone near the prow. Rocks were then placed on top of and around the ship, and these in turn were covered by a colossal mound of peat turves. The enormous weight of the mound – estimated at 6,000 tons – gradually caused the base of the grave to collapse and the resultant subsidence badly crushed the ship. (Steve Noon © Osprey Publishing Ltd)

of the ribs by means of trenails. The *meginhúfr* also acts as a point of contact for the crossbeams, which span the ribs. These are supported by vertical props that are mortised to the underside of the beams and cut to fit over the ribs below. The 11th and 12th strakes are secured by rivets to knees, which in turn are riveted to each end of the crossbeams and further strengthen the ship's hull. The 12th strake forms the gunwale and is pierced with 15 circular oar holes. Each of these has an upward, aft-facing slot through which the blade of an oar can pass, allowing the oars to be put out from the inside of the ship. No slot exists in the hole nearest to the bow, however, as the narrow structure of the ship would not allow an oar to be manoeuvred from the inside. The oar holes are unshuttered, an indication that the ship was never intended to weather heavy seas.

The shield rack is formed by a thin pine batten that runs along the outside face of the gunwale. It is held in place by a number of projecting cleats that create a series of gaps into which the ship's shields could be slotted. This is

Viking head, from a carving on the 9th-century Oseberg wagon frame. Like all surviving contemporary representations of Vikings, he is moustached and bearded. (Werner Forman Archive / Viking Ship Museum, Bygdoy)

arranged in such a way so as not to cover the oar holes and means the ship could be rowed with the shields in place.

The ship's decking is constructed from pine planking between 2 and 3 centimetres (0.8 and 1.2 inches) thick. With the exception of the planks at the bow and stern and on each side of the mast, the decking is nailed fast to the crossbeams. Such limited access to the space below decks further reinforces the theory that the ship was not designed for long and arduous voyages.

The mast is of pine and is estimated to have been 12–13 metres (39–43 feet) high. The keelson, in which the boot of the mast rests, lies over the keel but is not attached to it. Short and relatively insubstantial for a vessel this size, it extends over only two of the ship's ribs and is supported on each side by two cleats. The socket that accommodates the mast has a rounded fore section, while aft it is cut square, a simple but ingenious feature that facilitates

The ship depicted on this 8th-century picture stone from Tjängvide, Gotland, bears a striking resemblance to the Oseberg ship, an indication perhaps that the royal burial vessel was not unique and that ships of a similar design existed in other parts of Scandinavia. Note the shallow freeboard and the ubiquitous chequered sail. (Antivarisk-Topografiska Arkivet, National Heritage Board, Stockholm)

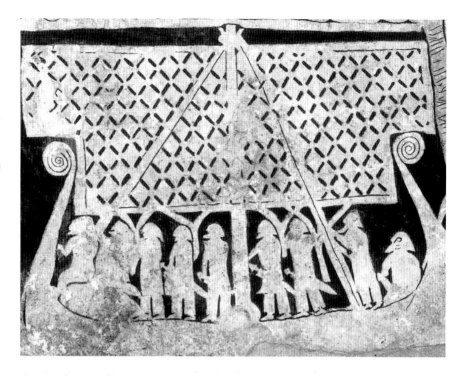

the raising and lowering of the mast, but gives it a secure seating when under sail. Immediately in front of this socket, the timber of the keelson rises in a vertical arm, which not only guides the mast into the socket, but also acts as a brace where it leaves the keelson and passes through the mast-fish at deck level. Although it extends over four crossbeams, the mast-fish, like the keelson, is quite a frail structure. In an attempt to strengthen it, the mast-fish is formed in an arch running fore to aft, and is supported by the crossbeam in front of the mast, which curves up above deck level to meet it. This arrangement, while giving heightened support to the mast, had only proved partially successful, as the mast-fish had cracked, presumably from the strain exerted upon it when the ship was under sail, and had been repaired with two iron bands. While the fore-end of the mast-fish is closed and solid, there is a deep groove aft, in which the mast would rest when lowered. When the mast was raised, the groove would be filled by a tightly fitting oak chock.

A long piece of timber measuring 12.5 metres (41 feet) was found with the ship, and, based on its proportions, some believed it to be a yard. A rakke, which would have held it to the mast, was also discovered. No sail, however, was found with the Oseberg ship, and any notions as to rigging arrangements can only be tentative. Fore and back stays were almost certainly employed to raise, support and lower the mast, and although there is no evidence of permanent fixtures for supporting shrouds, these may have been secured through holes that had been bored through the ship's knees. No doubt cordage from the yard and the lower corners of the sail, the clews, was fastened to cleats fixed aft of the third and fourth ribs.

The oak rudder is attached to the ship's starboard side by means of a flexible withy, in this case of pine roots, that is threaded through the rudder and the conical outboard block, then lashed inboard through three holes bored in the rudder rib. The neck of the rudder is held in place at the gunwale by a plaited leather band. In order to withstand the considerable strain caused while operating the rudder, the gunwale is reinforced at this point by a solid block of oak that tapers gracefully towards the stern. There was, however, no trace of a tiller.

Fifteen pairs of oars were also found on board the ship. They vary in length from between 3.7 and 4.03 metres (12.1 and 13.2 feet) in order to accommodate the curve of the ship's hull and the varying distances to the waterline. The looms feature delicately painted designs and taper to finely bevelled, leaf-shaped blades. When not in use they would be stored in the two pairs of large wooden forks attached inboard to each side of the ship.

Though beautifully made and perfectly functional, neither the oars nor the rudder showed any signs of wear and had obviously never been used. As we are fairly certain that the ship had already been retired from use at the time of the burial, it is more than probable that some of its original fittings had been stripped for use on other vessels, and that the rudder and oars were replacements made specifically for the funeral.

Because there is no evidence of fixed rowing benches on board, we can assume that the crew sat on sea chests to row. The dimensions of at least one chest on the ship make it ideally suited to such a purpose; even the iron nails used in its construction have tin-plated heads to protect against tarnishing from salt water spray. The ship is equipped with a well-preserved iron anchor about 1 metre (3.3 feet) long and weighing just under 10 kilograms (22 pounds). Along with its oak anchor stock, it is fitted with two rings to accommodate cables, one at the top of its shaft, the other between its flukes. Though gracefully made, it is very slight and on its own would never hold fast a ship of this size. One theory has it that when the ship was made fast ashore, such an anchor would be used to keep it clear of land or other vessels.

A pine gangplank nearly 7 metres (23 feet) long and 30 centimetres (11.8 inches) wide was also found. There is a hole at one end for securing it to the ship, and the upper surface is deeply ridged to assist purchase. The ship was also equipped with a long-handled baler, buckets, a large copper cauldron for cooking and a water cask.

Finally we come to the magnificent prow and stern. Formed in lavishly carved, soaring arches, they tower 5 metres (16.4 feet) above the waterline and terminate in elegant, serpentine spirals. Not only do they give the Oseberg ship its essential character, they also confirm its status as the finest expression of artistic endeavour yet discovered from the Viking Age. Both sides of the prow and stern are decorated with a frieze of fabulous beasts. Typical of the style of the period, the carving is of the highest order. At the point where the arch becomes a spiral, the design becomes simpler, the lines imitating a serpent's body and terminating in the creature's head at the prow and its tail at the stern.

Where the transition to prow and stern begins, the gunwales — which at this point are made from beechwood, the only part of the ship's structure that is not oak — broaden as they rise and feature panels carved with the same beasts that decorate the prow and stern. These sections are known as *brander*, and inside the sharp angle created where they meet are two braces carved in the same style. The upper of the two is triangular and is known as the *tingl* while the lower, a transverse bar, is known as the *spån*.

Clearly, elements of the Oseberg ship's construction would have prevented it from safely crossing the open sea. Some scholars have attributed this frailty to the kind of tentative design that might be expected in a transitional stage of development, and there may well be some truth in this. It has been proven, however, that before the Oseberg ship was even built, Viking shipbuilders had already developed vessels that were quite capable of crossing the North Sea, as monks on Lindisfarne found out to their cost in AD 793. It would appear, then, that the Oseberg ship was built specifically for short, fair-weather voyages in Norway's sheltered waterways and that a more robust construction had perhaps been sacrificed to create a spacious pleasure craft to be used on special occasions — a luxury status symbol for a queen.

The Gokstad ship

Although lacking the more intricate decoration of the Oseberg ship, the Gokstad ship is still a masterpiece of the Viking shipwright's art. With its hallmark design of uncluttered lines and rustic accuracy, the Gokstad ship remains one of the most seaworthy vessels ever built.

The ship lay under a mound 43.5 metres (142.7 feet) in diameter and 5 metres (16.4 feet) high near the Gokstad farm in Vestfold, not far from Oseberg. It was excavated in 1880 by Nicolay Nicolyasen, and although the grave had been plundered in antiquity, the ship was found to be in a remarkable state of preservation due to the damp blue clay that surrounded it. The burial chamber had been erected aft of the mast and contained the skeleton of a powerfully built man in his early 60s. He had been well equipped for his last journey, being accompanied by 12 horses, six dogs and, most interestingly, a peacock — the presence of which indicates far-flung voyaging or exotic trade connections.

Although the ship was built around AD 890, the basic method of construction remains the same as that employed 90 years earlier in the Oseberg vessel. Both ships are in the *karvi* class and were designed primarily for coastal voyaging, but several important differences had evolved that allowed the Gokstad ship to cross the North Sea and even the Atlantic in relative safety.

With the exception of the pine decking, the Gokstad ship is built throughout of oak. The vessel is somewhat larger than the Oseberg ship, being 23.24 metres (76.3 feet) long with a maximum width amidships of 5.25 metres (17.2 feet). The weight of the ship, fully equipped, is estimated at 20.2 metric tons (22.2 US tons). The clinker-built hull consists of 16 strakes on each side, four more than the Oseberg ship, making the height from the base of the keel to the gunwale amidships 1.95 metres (6.4 feet), and giving the Gokstad ship a considerably higher freeboard and more rounded transverse profile than the Oseberg vessel. The keel itself is radially cut from a straight-grown oak, measures 17.6 metres (57.7 feet) long and is fashioned in a similar manner to that in the Oseberg ship, in a flat, even arch. It is, however, significantly deeper, being 37 centimetres (14.6 inches) high amidships, increasing to 40 centimetres (15.8 inches) at the bow and 42 centimetres (16.5 inches) at the stern. T-shaped in transverse section, the bottom edge amidships is 13 centimetres (5.1 inches) wide and tapers towards the bow and stern, while the upper projecting ridge is 20 centimetres (7.9 inches) wide and provides a broad, stable base for the hull. Even in heavy seas, such a sturdy, well-balanced keel would allow the ship to perform a wide range of manoeuvres while under sail and would reduce the chances of swamping or capsizing.

Fore and aft, the keel is scarfed to two transitional pieces, which in turn are secured by scarf joints to the prow and stern. Here, the projecting upper ridge of the keel transforms into a rabbet to which each of the strakes is secured. The upper sections of both the prow and stern are incomplete – they protruded above the bed of clay in which the ship rested and, as a consequence, perished with the passage of time. Although we cannot be sure how they terminated, it is noticeable at the bow and stern that the inner curve is interrupted by a sharply rising section, while the outer edge follows on in the same graceful line, possibly making the stem and stern posts wider as they rose to their points of termination. It is equally possible, however, that the prow and stern terminated in a point, which would have been formed if the shipwright followed the sheer strake into the rear edge of the stem and stern.

From the keel, the first nine strakes below the waterline are flexible, being generally 2.6 centimetres (1.02 inches) thick. The garboard strake is nailed to

A masterpiece of construction, it is difficult to imagine how Viking shipbuilders could have improved on such a timeless design as the Gokstad ship. Note the ship's roomy interior and the transitional piece where the keel meets the prow. (University Museum of Cultural Heritage, University of Oslo, Norway)

the keel, and by means of their integral pierced cleats, strakes two to eight are lashed to the ribs with fine spruce roots, while the ninth strake is secured to the ribs by trenails. The transitional tenth strake, the *meginhúfr*, is 4.4 centimetres (1.7 inches) thick amidships and is also fastened to the ribs and crossbeams with trenails. The Gokstad ship has 19 ribs, all hewn from naturally curved oak limbs. The last ribs fore and aft are fashioned as bulkheads, their sides cut in steps, enabling a flush fit where they are nailed to the ship's strakes. The bottom section of each bulkhead is pierced to allow drainage, the bulkhead aft also serving as the securing point for the rudder withy.

The crossbeams, which span the ribs, are arched on their undersides in order to provide maximum support for the *meginhúfr*, their ends obliquely flushcut where they meet the ship's sides. The crossbeams are further supported by a series of vertical props, while amidships, some are supported by the structure that braces and holds the mast.

Carrying the weight of the mast, the keelson on the Gokstad ship is a sturdy piece of timber that rests over the keel and over four of the ship's ribs. It is 3.75 metres (12.3 feet) long, 40 centimetres (15.8 inches) high and 60 centimetres (23.6 inches) wide amidships, tapering fore and aft. As in the Oseberg ship, it is not attached to the keel, but in this case is nailed on each side via substantial knees to the eighth, tenth and 11th ribs from the stern. The

The Gokstad ship. The Gokstad ship was found with 64 shields in situ, 32 lining each of her sides and painted alternatively black and yellow. The figure head is based on an animal-headed post found among the Gokstad grave furnishings. Note the spears stored at the stern and the weather-vane, both of which follow examples on a picture stone from Smiss, Stenkyrka, in Gotland. (Steve Noon © Osprey Publishing Ltd)

design of the mast-socket follows that of the Oseberg ship and, forward of the tenth rib and the socket, features the same strong, vertically inclined arm, which also supports the tenth beam.

At deck level, the mast-fish had to be strong enough to brace a pine mast 30 centimetres (11.8 inches) thick and an estimated 13 metres (42.7 feet) high. Accordingly, it is the largest single component in the ship and is much more robust than that in the Oseberg vessel. Cut from a solid block of oak and weighing around 4 tons (4.4 US tons), it is steeply arched, tapering fore and aft to its characteristic fish-tailed shape. It is approximately 5 metres (16.4 feet) long and spans six crossbeams, into which it is mortised. At its centre it is 1 metre (3.3 feet) wide, 42 centimetres (16.5 inches) thick and on each side is made fast to the crossbeams by way of four substantial knees. The mast-fish is further supported by the ninth crossbeam, which, formed like a vertical plank, is supported by the rib below it. As in the Oseberg ship, the

The interior of the Gokstad ship. In the foreground is the huge mast-fish with the mast-lock in place. Note the robust, curved knees that secure it to the beams. The oar holes and their shutters can be seen on each side of the hull along with the knees and top-ribs that support the upper strakes. Note the rebates in the crossbeams to accommodate the loose decking. To the right of the mast-fish are oars, a gangplank, spars and, between two knees, the beiti-ass block. Note also the shield rack fixed to the gunwale and the two T-shaped posts on which the oars would have rested when not in use. (© University Museum of Cultural Heritage, University of Oslo, Norway, photographer Schwitter)

mast-fish is forked aft, forming a slot into which the lowered mast could rest. When raised, the slot could be plugged by a remarkably tight wedge – all in all, a firm and secure supporting structure for the mast.

As befitting an ocean-going vessel, the Gokstad ship is high sided, having six strakes above the waterline. The first four of these are braced inboard by strong knees to which they are trenailed, the knees themselves being nailed fast to the crossbeams. The first three of these strakes are about 2.6 centimetres (1.02 inches) thick, the fourth being slightly thicker at 3.2 centimetres (1.26 inches) in order to accommodate the oar holes. There are 16 of these on each side, one pair between each of the ship's ribs, excepting the space between the extreme ribs fore and aft. The ribs are spaced 1 metre (3.3 feet) apart, thus allowing the perfect distance in which to produce the maximum oar stroke. The oar holes are about 40 centimetres (15.8 inches) above the decking; as there is no evidence of rowing benches, and assuming that the oarsmen sat on sea chests, this would be a comfortable height at which to pull oars. The oar

The full-sized Gokstad replica Gaia. Based at Sandefjord, Norway, Gaia was built in 1989–90 and is regularly sailed in Scandinavian waters. Reaching speeds of up to 17 knots, she has also voyaged across the Atlantic to North America. (Keith Durham)

holes, like those in the Oseberg ship, are slotted to allow oar blades to be deployed from the inside of the ship, but on the Gokstad ship they can be closed by means of neatly contrived, circular wooden shutters, a sure sign that this ship was expected to cope in rough seas.

Above the 14th strake the two uppermost strakes are trenailed to a series of additional top ribs, one for every other knee. For additional support, these ribs are butted into the gunwale and also extend down over the previous three strakes, to which they are firmly nailed. Immediately below the gunwale inboard, a batten with 11 rectangular openings between each rib runs along the ship's side and forms the shield rack. The Gokstad ship was found with 64 shields, which were tied in place to the shield rack with bast cords. Covering the oar holes and painted alternatively black and yellow, there are 32 on each side of the ship, two overlapping shields to each oar hole. Although the sagas decree that sailing with shields hung out in this manner was at variance with tradition, many depictions of ships on the Gotland picture stones seem to contradict such advice.

Also present on the upper strakes and secured inboard are three pairs of wooden cleats. These are spaced on both sides of the ship between the first and fourth ribs from the stern and would no doubt have served as convenient points for making fast the braces, sheets and other cordage that constituted the ship's rigging.

Unlike the Oseberg ship, the pine decking planks are not nailed down, but rest snugly on the crossbeams, which are rebated to receive them. This arrangement allows all the space beneath deck to be easily accessed for baling and for the storage of weapons and provisions, and is a further indication that the ship was designed with long-range voyaging in mind. Immediately above deck level and forward of the mast inboard, there are on each side of the ship two rectangular blocks fixed securely between the seventh and eighth rib from the bow. They are deeply recessed, and for many years their significance remained a mystery. It is now apparent that they served as supports for a spar or *beiti-ass*, the base of which could be jammed into the recess at a variety of angles, the top being lodged wherever appropriate on the ship's sail, keeping it taut and maximizing the spread of canvas when tacking. No sail was found on board, but based on the likely dimensions of the mast and yard, it has been estimated at 70 square metres (754 square feet). A number of spars were found, along with some cordage, blocks and tackle, but we can only make educated guesses as to rigging arrangements.

Apart from its sailing activities, the strength of the Gokstad ship lay in its oar power. The design of the hull is such that the gunwale runs parallel to the waterline for most of its length, thus allowing the maximum number of oars to strike the water in unison, and whether engaged in piracy or raiding, the speed generated by 32 powerful, experienced oarsmen would have given a substantial advantage over pursuing forces or lesser craft. As the ship is quite capable of carrying 60 or 70 men – a double crew – it is likely that while half rested, the others rowed. The oars, which were discovered in the bow, range in length from 5.3 to 5.85 metres (17.4 to 19.2 feet) to suit their station on board ship. Made of pine, they have slender looms that taper towards the handles and small, lancet-shaped blades.

Also above deck level are three T-shaped posts. One of these is situated midway between the mast and stern and another midway between the mast and prow. These two extend below deck to the keel, where they are secured by two cleats. The third post, immediately in front of the mast, is nailed securely to the mast-fish. The three posts are about 2.4 metres (7.9 feet) high above the deck and a little over 4 metres (13.1 feet) apart. As we have seen, the ship's oars have an average length of about 5.5 metres (18 feet) and it is fairly certain that when not in use the oars, and perhaps the yard, would have been stored across these posts, keeping them well clear of the deck.

At the stern there is a small raised poop-deck for the helmsman, and fitted starboard aft is the ship's blade-like rudder. Cut from a single piece of oak, it is 3.3 metres (10.8 feet) high, and 42 centimetres (16.5 inches) wide. It also extends 50 centimetres (19.7 inches) below the keel amidships and would have helped prevent sideways slippage when tacking. The lower aft edge terminates in a slight curved heel and is fitted with a small metal clamp. To this would have been tied a rope that would have allowed the rudder to be raised while in shallow water. The rudder is attached to the ship in the same manner as in the Oseberg vessel, though where it is in contact with the hull, strengthening measures have been considerably increased. The strain on the rudder withy can be quite severe when the wind is to starboard, and when to port, the band around the rudder neck can also experience considerable strain. To counter this, a solid oak block pointing aft has also been nailed to the rudder rib and to the ship's side inboard, where the rudder withy passes through the hull. In addition, where the rudder band passes inboard, a stout plank 10 centimetres (3.9 inches) thick is nailed to the gunwale outboard and to the strake below it. The rudder neck extends about 50 centimetres (19.7 inches) above the gunwale and is fitted with a detachable tiller. This is the only decorated object on the ship and features a small, gaping dragon's head, highlighted in yellow paint and in the act of devouring the spigot.

The ship had been fitted out with an anchor estimated at 1.1 metres (3.6 feet) long, a pine gangplank 7.4 metres (24.3 feet) in length and a cask that would hold 750 litres (198 gallons) of fresh water. Also interred with the ship

This small boat, built in the Museum shipyard at Roskilde, is a replica of one of the three boats interred with the Gokstad ship. Lightly constructed, it shares the same gracious lines as the parent ship. In parts of Scandinavia, similar vessels are in use to this day. (Keith Durham)

were three exquisite smaller boats, six collapsible beds, a tent with decorated verge boards, a large bronze pot and various kitchen utensils.

Any doubts as to the seaworthiness of the Gokstad ship were dispelled in 1893 when a faithfully copied replica, the *Viking*, under the command of Captain Magnus Andersen, sailed 3,000 miles from Bergen to the United States for the Chicago World Fair. Crossing the Atlantic in varying weather conditions, without mishap and in just 27 days, Captain Andersen was delighted by the way his ship performed. Admiring its flexibility, he wrote:

> the bottom as well as the keel could therefore yield to the movements of the ship and in a heavy head sea it would rise and fall as much as ¾ inch [1.9 centimetres]. But strangely enough the ship was watertight all the same. Its elasticity was apparent also in other ways. In a heavy sea the gunnel would twist up to 6 inches [15.2 centimetres] out of line. All this elasticity, combined with fine lines, naturally made for speed, and we often had the pleasure of darting through the water at speeds of 10, and sometimes even 11 knots. This in spite of a primitive and relatively small rigging.

He was full of praise too for the side rudder, which he described as 'nothing short of brilliant'.

Though larger and more specialized vessels would be built in the 11th century, such testimonies ensure that the impressive vessel discovered at Gokstad reigns supreme as the classic Viking ship.

SHIPBUILDING IN THE 11TH CENTURY

As we have seen in the Gokstad ship, Viking shipbuilders were well able to construct a single vessel that would meet the needs of both pirate and trader. However, due to a unique salvage operation at Skuldelev on Roskilde Fjord in Denmark, we know that by the year AD 1000, a marked distinction had been established between warships and merchantmen, and that construction methods had evolved accordingly.

In 1962, Danish archaeologists uncovered and retrieved the submerged remains of five very different kinds of vessels, which in the 11th century had been scuttled in a narrow stretch of the fjord, creating an underwater blockade to thwart a seaborne incursion on the thriving town of Roskilde. A showcase of Viking shipbuilding skills, the find consisted of a longship (*skei*), a small warship (*snekkja*), a coastal trader, a small cargo boat and an ocean-going merchant ship (*knarr*), all of which shared the same basic construction.

The ships were still clinker built, but shipwrights had dispensed with the system of lashing the ship's strakes to the ribs in favour of trenails, by which they were now secured, thus creating a more rigid structure. The mast-fish too had disappeared, being replaced by a strong crossbeam, which was pitched higher than its fellows, supporting the mast and bracing the ship's sides, to which it was secured by vertical and horizontal knees. Above the waterline, top ribs had also disappeared, and for most of their length, the upper strakes were now reinforced by longitudinal stringers. The crossbeams were still secured by trenails to the tops of the ribs and by knees to the sides of the hull. Also, some of the ships had additional crossbeams permanently secured above deck level, which would have accommodated oarsmen.

The small coastal trader also yielded intact a slender and skilfully fashioned prow. Hewn from a single piece of timber, its carved lines follow the form of the curving strakes, which meet it and imitate their clinker-built construction. It is interesting to note that in addition to oak, a variety of wood types such as lime, ash, willow, birch and pine have been used in the construction of these vessels, an indication that perhaps even then, suitable oaks were becoming hard to find.

The longships

By the beginning of the 11th century, Scandinavian monarchs began building large warships and instigated the *ledungen*, by which every district under the king's domain was obliged to build ships for the sole purpose of warfare and to provide militia to crew them. The primary function of these ships, large and small, was to transport as many fighting men as possible to a point of conflict and to do it rapidly, without having to rely on favourable winds. This gave rise to the true

An English longship as portrayed on the Bayeux Tapestry. Note the kite-shaped shields hung inboard and the break in the gunwale line, which may have facilitated loading. The mast is supported by shrouds, a fore stay and a back stay. Note the carved prow and stern, and the man at the bow, who uses a depth stick. The ship tows a boat similar to those found in the Gokstad burial. (The Bayeux Tapestry — 11th century. By special permission of the City of Bayeux)

Viking warships or *langskips*. Long and narrow, often with a length–breadth ratio of 7:1, their speed while under sail or being propelled by large numbers of warriors/oarsmen, was formidable. Lightly constructed and designed primarily for use in Scandinavian coastal waters they were, as we shall see, equally at home on the North Sea or Baltic. Longships varied considerably in size and tended to be classified by the number of spaces between deck beams (*rum*) or the number of paired rowing places (*sessa*), making a ship with 30 oars a *Fimtansessa* (15-bencher). The 10th-century Gulathing Law tells us that a *threttansessa* – a ship with 26 oars – was the smallest that could be 'counted by benches', indicating that smaller vessels were unsuitable for military purposes. The majority of Scandinavian levy ships appear to have been 20- or 25-benchers, but smaller ships were undoubtedly called into use when the need arose. In a bid to challenge the Viking raids of the late 9th century, the *Anglo-Saxon Chronicle* tells us that Alfred the Great built ships of 30 or more benches, 'almost twice as long' as Viking vessels, indicating that it was 15- and 16-benchers, such as the Gokstad ship, which at that time carried Viking raiders to England.

Near the end of the 10th century a number of giant longships, or *drekar*, emerged, including King Olav Tryggvasson's *Long Serpent*, which sported 34 benches. In AD 1062, Harald Hardrada launched a 35-bencher appropriately named *Great Dragon*. It is described as being 'much broader than normal warships; it was of the same size and proportions as the *Long Serpent* and each part was built with great care. On the stem was a dragon-head, and on the stern a dragon-tail and the bows of the ship were gilded. It had 35 pairs of rowing benches and was large [even] for that size of vessel.' The first longship to be discovered, however, was somewhat smaller.

Page from the 16th-century version of the Jonsbok, *the law code brought to Iceland from Norway. This marginal illustration shows a longship at sea, and the text refers to the law code and arrangements for freight handling. (Werner Forman Archive/Stofnun Arna Magnussonar a Islandi, Reykjavik, Iceland)*

Ship construction, 11th century

This prow (1), hewn from a single block of timber, is carved to follow the lines of the ship's strakes, which it is rebated to receive. Note the dragon-head from the *Helge Ask* and the manner of attachment to the prow. The method of construction that had been established by the 11th century (2) used trenails to secure the strakes to the ribs. Note the upper crossbeams, or thwarts, which could serve as benches for oarsmen, and above the keelson, the sturdy mast-beam.

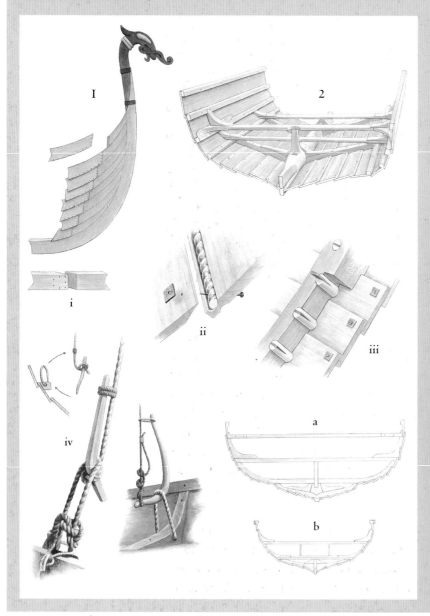

Left to right: (i) scarf joint, (ii) rove, rivet and tarred rope, (iii) rib, clinker-built strakes and trenails. (iv) shows two kinds of shroud-pin or *vantnåle* and the manner in which they are used to secure the shrouds to the hull.

Cross sections of (a) Skudelev 1, a deep-sided ocean-going *knarr* and (b) Skudelev 5, a small, narrow warship. (Steve Noon © Osprey Publishing Ltd)

The Skuldelev 5 replica Helge Ask on Roskilde Fjord. Her hull is painted yellow and red in the style of ships depicted in the Bayeux Tapestry and she is doubtless representative of many of them. (Photo Ole Malling, The Viking Ship Museum, Roskilde)

The Ladby ship

This ship, found in 1935, was unearthed from a chieftain's burial mound on the island of Funen in Denmark. Only the ghostly imprint of the ship remained, the impression of the hull being marked by rusted nails and dark stains in the soil. The vessel proved to be 21.54 metres (70.67 feet) long and only 2.92 metres (9.58 feet) wide amidships, a length–breadth ratio of 7:1. Compare this to the Gokstad ship's ratio of 4.5:1 and we have a predatory, rapier-like craft with a very shallow draught, the height from the keel to the gunwale being just 1.02 metres (3.35 feet). Undoubtedly a warship, the vessel was fitted with a dragon-head, evident from a surviving crest of iron spirals at the ship's prow.

Four large iron rings were also found attached to the ship's ribs amidships and were probably used to secure the shrouds. Academics were sceptical about the seaworthiness of such a vessel and confined its activities to coastal waters, a theory roundly disproved when the Danes built a replica of the ship, the *Imme Gram,* and sailed her across the North Sea.

The striking dragon head affixed to the Helge Ask. *Icelandic law decreed that such figureheads were removed when approaching land, so as not to offend benign earth spirits. (Keith Durham)*

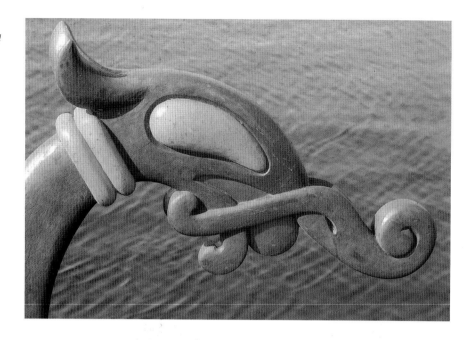

The Skuldelev warships

Sharing the same length–breadth ratio, but dating from around AD 1030, the small Skuldelev warship known as Skuldelev 5 is 17.3 metres (56.8 feet) long and 2.5 metres (8.2 feet) wide. Construction follows the 11th-century pattern, the hull comprising 16 ribs and seven strakes on each side, the first four being oak, the upper three, ash. Each rib is spanned by a crossbeam that supports a deck of loose planking level with the top of the third strake. In order to provide benches for oarsmen a second set of narrow beams was secured 30 centimetres (11.8 inches) above 13 of the lower beams, the top strake being pierced with a like number of oar holes on each side.

There is a marked economy in the ship's construction, which is evident in the upper three strakes. These have been stripped from a similar vessel, inappropriate oar holes patched and new ones cut about 95 centimetres (37.4 inches) apart to suit the rowing benches. Other repairs are also noticeable, and this kind of penny-pinching indicates that the ship was probably built and maintained as part of Roskilde's *ledungen* obligation. Traces of a shield rack were also found running along the edge of the gunwale. Carrying a crew of 30 warriors, a sail estimated at 45 square metres (484 square feet) and deploying 26 oars, this vessel was a fine warship and is no doubt representative of many of the ships depicted on the Bayeux Tapestry.

Along with other ships from the Skuldelev find, a full-scale replica of Skudelev 5, the *Helge Ask*, has been constructed by a skilled team of scholars, craftsmen and

sailors based at the Viking Ship Museum at Roskilde. Using sound archaeological data and traditional methods of construction, the team relies strictly on tools copied from examples from the Viking period, and by building these replicas and taking them out to sea, they have greatly enhanced our knowledge of Viking ships and seafaring.

Under a good breeze and utilizing a sail of 50 square metres (538 square feet), the *Helge Ask* has reached speeds of 14 knots, and under oar power, even when rowing into the wind, can make a respectable 5.5 knots.

Skuldelev 2, the other warship that was part of the underwater blockade, is a true longship, or *skei*. Built of oak, the ship is estimated to have been approximately 30 metres (98 feet) long and 3.8 metres (12.5 feet) wide. The ship's strakes, 12 on each side, were only 2–2.5 centimetres (0.79–0.98 inches) thick, and the keelson,

Much has been learned from experimental archaeology, and here horses are being transported in the Ladby ship replica Imme Gram, *giving credibility to similar scenes depicted in the Bayeux Tapestry. (Photo Ole Crumlin-Pedersen, The Viking Ship Museum, Roskilde)*

Havhingsten fra Glendalough. *Launched in 2004 at Roskilde, this splendid reconstruction of the vessel known as Skuldelev 2 gives us a vivid idea of the awesome appearance of a true Viking longship. The name translates as 'Sea Stallion from Glendalough', in recognition of the original ship's Irish ancestry. She was capable of carrying 70-80 warriors/oarsmen, and with a draught of only 1 metre (3.3 feet), could strike deep into enemy territory. (Photo Werner Karrasch, The Viking Ship Museum, Roskilde)*

at 13.34 metres (43.8 feet) long, had obviously been fashioned to give longitudinal strength to the hull. Fully crewed, the ship would have held 60 to 100 men and was fitted with between 56 and 60 oars. Under oar power, even over great distances, this ship would have been able to maintain impressive speeds of 5–6 knots. Her sail has been estimated at between 118–120 square metres (1270–1292 square feet), which with a following wind would have achieved speeds in the region of 20 knots. For all her great length, this awesome longship still retains a draught of only 1 metre (3.3 feet), allowing her to cruise the same shallow waters as much smaller craft.

That such great vessels were capable of crossing the open sea was proved beyond doubt when the ship's timbers were subjected to dendroanalysis. Tests confirmed that the ship had been built of Irish oak, probably in the Viking city of Dublin, around the year AD 1042, and had made at least one voyage across the North Sea to Denmark.

Although only 25 per cent of the original ship was preserved, among the 1,800 fragments recovered was the entire keelson. Fortunately, the sternpost had also survived, along with some strake fragments that were attached to it, up to the height of the gunwale. As the most crucial dimensions of the ship were preserved, the Viking Ship Museum made the decision to construct a full-size replica of the longship known as Skuldelev 2.

Work on the reconstruction began in 2000. Wood from around 340 trees was used in the ship's construction, along with 400 kilograms (882 pounds)

Another view of Havhingsten fra Glendalough. *(Keith Durham)*

of iron, which was used to manufacture the ship's 7,000 nails. Linden bast, horsehair and hemp were used in the manufacture of the ship's 2,000 metres (6,562 feet) of cordage and the 118-square-metre (1270-square-feet) sail was manufactured from flax.

In September 2004, after four years of hard work, a magnificent, full-scale replica of Skuldelev 2 was launched with much ceremony at the Viking Ship Museum's harbour. Since the launch, the ship has undergone extensive sea trials in Danish coastal waters and will be tested in the North Sea in preparation for a voyage to Dublin, scheduled for 2007.

Skuldelev 2 was, until 1997, the longest ship found from the Viking Age. Then the remains of another nine ships were discovered sunk in mud, alongside the actual Viking Ship Museum. One of them, Roskilde 6, has been identified as a longship, being an incredible 36 metres (118 feet) long and 3.5 metres (11.5 feet) wide, putting it firmly into the class of vessels which gave rise to the *Long Serpent* and *Great Dragon*. Built around AD 1025, such a splendid ship would almost certainly be the property of royalty, and it is tempting to link the find to King Cnut, who then ruled Denmark, Norway, England and southern Sweden.

The oak keel, T-shaped in cross section and 32 metres (105 feet) long, consisted of a central section and two end pieces, to which it was well secured by long scarf joints. Regularly spaced ribs 78 centimetres (30.7 inches) apart covered the first five strakes, making the upper crossbeams (which have unfortunately not survived) an ideal distance apart for rowing. Light half-frames secured between the ribs gave added support to the third and fourth strakes, the latter of which was strengthened by a stringer on to which the lower beams would have been attached. Only a fragment of the keelson has survived, and this rested on the ribs and was secured by horizontal knees.

The ship's sail has been estimated at 200 square metres (2153 square feet), and with its 78 rowing stations, this leviathan must have been a breathtaking sight. A true saga-ship, it could easily carry 100 warriors, and without doubt would have had its bellicose image enhanced by a fine dragon-headed prow.

War and peace on board the longship

As detailed in 'Tactics' (page 92), in formal naval engagements of the period, ships were roped together in a line, the centrepiece being the king's, or chieftain's, ship. Then, as at the battles of Hafrsfjord in AD 872 and Svöldr in AD 1000, these floating fighting-platforms drifted towards each other, while smaller warships from each side attempted to outflank the enemy line. To combat this, high-sided *knarrs* were often positioned at the ends of these lines, where they could rain down an assortment of missiles on to the smaller attacking vessels. As the opposing lines drew close amid a shower of arrows and spears, boarding parties would begin the attack, the object being to clear each successive enemy ship until a victor emerged.

Even in peacetime, there were few luxuries to be found on board these vessels. Other than on very fine days, baling must have been an almost continual task. In such open ships, men must have been regularly soaked through either by the weather or the waves, and finding somewhere decent to sleep must have been difficult, to say the least. While at sea, their diet would have consisted of dried fish and meat washed down with water, sour milk or beer. It is therefore not surprising that most crews, unless engaged in ocean-going travel, would make for shore as evening fell and pitch tent on dry land, where they could cook and sleep in relative comfort. Collapsible tents, cauldrons and portable cooking utensils were found on the Gokstad and Oseberg ships and were no doubt standard accessories on other ships, too. If a ship was anchored offshore, the sail could be spread over a collapsible frame, covering the deck amidships and providing rudimentary shelter for the crew.

The knarr

The westward expansion of the Norse in the 10th century necessitated the development of another type of vessel. By AD 870, the colonization of Iceland had begun, and between AD 985 and AD 986, Erik the Red led the first immigrants ashore on Greenland. Five years later, Leif Eriksson became the first European to set foot in North America (see 'Vikings in North America', page 65). Once settled in these somewhat barren North Atlantic outposts, colonists needed regular deliveries of essential supplies from their homelands, brought by ships that could also take their exports back to Scandinavia. The ships that

made these epic voyages 'west-over-sea' were *havskips* or *knarrs*, the most seaworthy vessels the Norsemen ever produced. High-sided and broad of beam, these vessels relied almost solely on a large rectangular sail for propulsion. In order to weather the heavy seas of the North Atlantic, they were constructed in a suitably robust manner.

Built between AD 1030 and AD 1050, Skuldelev 1 is a prime example of such a vessel, between 60 and 70 per cent of it being recovered from the underwater blockade. Dendroanalysis has shown that the ship was built in western Norway, probably on the Sognefjord, and was repaired in Oslo Fjord before sailing to Denmark.

The ship is 16.3 metres (53.5 feet) in length and has a width amidships of 4.5 metres (14.8 feet), the height from the keel to the gunwale being 2.1 metres (6.9 feet). When fully loaded, the ship's draught would be 1.3 metres (4.3 feet). The oak keel is 12.1 metres (39.7 feet) long, and the sternpost comprised three separate, scarfed pieces. The upper section, which received strakes six to 12, was fashioned in a similar way to the prow on Skuldelev 3, being carved in a fashion that continues the lines of the strakes. The ship's hull is formed by 12 pine strakes on each side, the fifth from the keel being steeply pitched and marking the transition between bottom and side.

The Skuldelev 1 replica Ottar under construction at the Museum shipyard, Roskilde. Note the cavernous cargo hold, the curving ribs and the sturdy crossbeams that brace her hull. (Photo Werner Karrasch, The Viking Ship Museum, Roskilde)

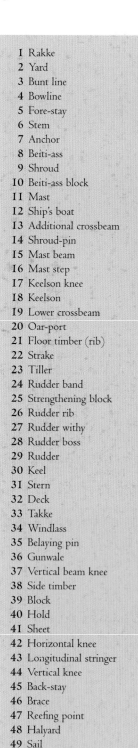

1 Rakke
2 Yard
3 Bunt line
4 Bowline
5 Fore-stay
6 Stem
7 Anchor
8 Beiti-ass
9 Shroud
10 Beiti-ass block
11 Mast
12 Ship's boat
13 Additional crossbeam
14 Shroud-pin
15 Mast beam
16 Mast step
17 Keelson knee
18 Keelson
19 Lower crossbeam
20 Oar-port
21 Floor timber (rib)
22 Strake
23 Tiller
24 Rudder band
25 Strengthening block
26 Rudder rib
27 Rudder withy
28 Rudder boss
29 Rudder
30 Keel
31 Stern
32 Deck
33 Takke
34 Windlass
35 Belaying pin
36 Gunwale
37 Vertical beam knee
38 Side timber
39 Block
40 Hold
41 Sheet
42 Horizontal knee
43 Longitudinal stringer
44 Vertical knee
45 Back-stay
46 Brace
47 Reefing point
48 Halyard
49 Sail
50 Mast-head

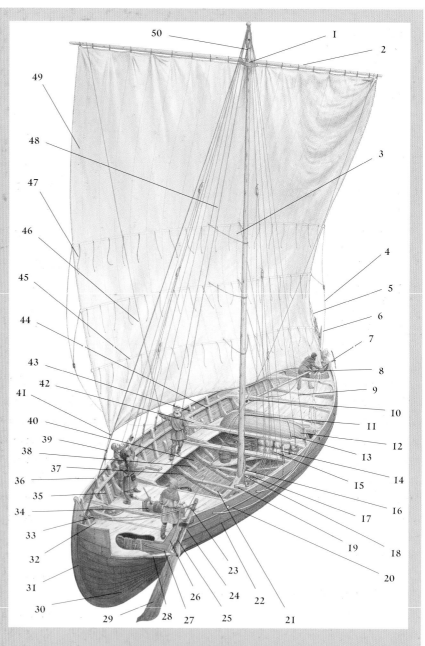

An 11th-century *knarr* as she would have appeared en route to Iceland. Note the exposed conditions that had to be endured on these long voyages by crew and passengers alike. A crew member deploys the *beiti-ass*. Note the ship's boat lashed across the cargo hold. In addition to cargo, Norse vessels would invariably carry some form of ballast. In order to show the interior of the ship clearly, this has been omitted from the illustration. (Steve Noon © Osprey Publishing Ltd)

The hull is strengthened by 14 ribs, with further support provided by additional ribs near the prow, stern and aft of the mast. Amidships is an open hold of 30–35 cubic metres (1059–1236 cubic feet) that would, it has been estimated, accommodate 24 tons (26.4 US tons) of cargo. Here, ribs extend over the first five strakes and crossbeams are fastened with massive knees that cover strakes six to 11 and, in places, 12. The keelson, which was over 5 metres (16 feet) long, extended over six ribs, the midship rib being immediately in front of the mast-step. Above this, at the level of the ninth strake, a sturdy crossbeam is secured to the knees over which it rests. This, and a robust additional beam above it, level with strake 11, would have helped to brace the mast. Four more of these top crossbeams were also evident, evenly spaced along the length of the ship. For additional longitudinal strength, the upper edge of strake 11 carried a sturdy stringer along its length, which featured horizontal knees on to which the upper crossbeams were secured.

The ship was decked fore and aft, and the crossbeams were rebated to receive the planking. About 3.5 metres (11.5 feet) forward of the mast at deck level on the port side, a *beiti-ass* block 1.25 metres (4 feet) long was found. The block had three well-used recesses cut into it and would have allowed a wide variety of angles for a spar when tacking. It has been estimated that the ship's sail would have been between 80 and 85 square metres (861 and 915 square feet), and that

The well-preserved remains of Skuldelev 1. On the forward port side note the surviving section of the longitudinal stringer rebated into the ribs, and below it, the beiti-ass block. (Photo Werner Karrasch, The Viking Ship Museum, Roskilde)

Launched in August 2000, the Ottar *is a fine example of an ocean-going knarr. Such a ship may well have been owned by a co-operative of merchants who would use her to transport their wares to northern trading emporiums such as Hedeby and Birka. (Keith Durham)*

she would have required between five and eight men to crew her. The *knarr* would have utilized two or four oars for manoeuvring, and may well have employed a windlass for raising and lowering the heavy yard. As such vessels were too heavy to be beached, a small ship's boat would have been towed or carried on board, in order to ferry cargo to and from shore.

A fine replica of Skuldelev I, the *Ottar*, has been built at Roskilde. Under sail in favourable conditions, the ship can easily cruise at 5–6 knots. With a strong following wind, however, she has reached maximum speeds of 12.5 to 13 knots.

Between the 10th and 12th centuries, when a *knarr* set out across the North Atlantic, it would be packed with a variety of livestock, provisions, timber, iron and whole families of immigrants and their belongings. As much dried food and fresh water as could be accommodated would be stored on board, for these ships were at the mercy of the wind, and depending on prevailing conditions, the duration of a voyage from Norway to Iceland could be between five and 20 days. Many ships, no matter how seaworthy, set out and were never seen again.

When Erik the Red sailed from Iceland to Greenland with 300 colonists in a total of 25 ships, only 14 of the ships reached their destination in safety: 'some were driven back and some were lost at sea'. Ships could also be blown wildly off course, though on occasion such calamities could lead to the sighting of new lands, as was the case with Bjarni Herjolfsson when he came across the coast of America in AD 986.

The compass was unknown, and when out of sight of land, the Norsemen would plot a course using the position of the sun and the stars. Much of their skill, however, lay in the observation of natural phenomena and a wide knowledge of the sea itself. Its varied colours would indicate where known currents ran, and the sighting of seabirds and marine life could also give clues as to their position. This kind of accumulated knowledge would be passed on to those who wished to follow, as is evident in these directions from the *Landnámabok* regarding the voyage from Norway to Greenland:

> From Hernor in Norway one is to keep sailing west for Hvarf in Greenland and then you will sail north of Shetland so that you can just sight it in very clear weather; but south of the Faroes so that the sea appears half-way up the mountain slopes; but on, south of Iceland so that you may have birds and whales from it.

Most of their sailing, however, was carried out within sight of the coasts and skerries of their homelands, and these coastal waters must have teemed with a wide variety of small cargo ships. One such vessel is the well-preserved wreck known as Skuldelev 3.

Built of oak around AD 1040 she is a small, elegant trading vessel 13.8 metres (45.3 feet) long, 3.3 metres (10.8 feet) wide amidships and has a draught of 85 centimetres (33.5 inches). She is decked fore and aft, leaving a large, open hold amidships with a volume of 10 cubic metres (353 cubic feet), which would have held about 4.5 tons (4.95 US tons) of cargo.

The keel, about 9 metres (29.5 feet) long, is scarfed with iron nails and trenails to the steeply rising stem and stern, the former of which is beautifully preserved. The hull consists of eight broad strakes on each side, the top four of which are strengthened along their upper edges by longitudinal stringers. The ship has 11 evenly spaced ribs and a triangular bulkhead at the bow, which features a stout knob to which an anchor or mooring rope could be attached. The ribs extend over the first four strakes and halfway across the fifth. The tops of the ribs support the first stringer, which lies flush with the upper edge of strake five, and supports the lower crossbeams. Knees secured to each end of the crossbeams support the second stringer, which in turn supports the upper crossbeams. These are rebated to receive the loose planking that forms the decking fore and aft. Upper crossbeams are absent amidships over the hold, except for the mast-beam, which is of a more robust construction than its fellows, and is secured to both the stringers and the hull by substantial horizontal and vertical knees.

The keelson is 3.7 metres (12 feet) long and spans three of the ship's ribs. It is deeply stepped to receive the mast, and the vertical mast support rising from it is firmly mortised into the mast-beam.

The well-preserved remains of the small coastal trader known as Skuldelev 3 have been the inspiration for a number of replicas. Such ships were the workhorses of the Viking era and would have plied Danish coastal waters and the Baltic. Note the reproduction prow, the original being carved from a single block of oak. (Photo Werner Karrasch, The Viking Ship Museum, Roskilde)

The gunwale is pierced with seven rectangular oar holes, two forward to starboard, three to port and one on each side aft of the hold. Oars would be used when manoeuvring the vessel, or over short distances when becalmed, but the primary means of propulsion was the sail. Much has been learned from Skuldelev 3 regarding rigging arrangements, as the gunwale features a number of holes that would have accommodated both standing and running rigging. Cleats were also found inboard and on each side of the gunwale outboard. Skuldelev 3 has been the inspiration for a number of replicas, notably *Roar Ege*, the first reconstruction to be undertaken at Roskilde and launched in 1984.

Under a sail of 45 square metres (484 square feet) and with a crew of five to eight people, this fine little ship has achieved speeds in excess of 8 knots, and when sailing at an angle into the wind, could beat at 60 degrees with a leeway of 5 to 6 degrees.

Roar Ege *moored beside her sister ship* Kraka Fyr *in the Museum harbour. Note the raised steerboard, the upper beams that can serve as rowing benches and, just visible, the ballast amidships. (Keith Durham)*

THE END OF THE LONGSHIP

By the mid-13th century, the growing strength and stability of the larger European kingdoms led to widespread commercial expansion. Profit became the driving force behind ship design and soon the cog, with its deep draught and massive cargo hold, began to replace the trusted *knarr*. Warships followed a similar path and the slim, predatory *langskips* were abandoned for high-sided vessels that sprouted wooden castles fore and aft. The age of the Viking ship was over.

Old habits die hard, however, and in remoter parts of the northern hemisphere many seafarers refused to abandon these elegant, seaworthy vessels simply because their time was past. As a consequence, until the end of the 19th century, traditionally built, north Norwegian *fembørings* and their hardy crews still plied the same, grey northern seas as did their forefathers a thousand years ago.

GLOSSARY

Aett: An extended family group; a clan.

Althing: A national assembly held for two weeks every summer.

Amidships: The centre of a vessel.

Amulet: An ornament or piece of jewellery worn for good luck and to ward off evil.

Beam: The width of a vessel.

Beiti-ass: A wooden spar used to tauten sail when tacking.

Berserker: A particularly fanatical (and perhaps psychotic) Viking warrior.

Bóndi: A land-owning freeman who had the right to bear arms and attend the Thing.

Boss: The metal guard covering the hand-grip of a shield.

Bowline: A line running from forward edge of sail to bow, which keeps sail taut.

Braces: Lines to control the angle of the yard in a vessel.

Bryti: A farm steward.

Burh: A Saxon stronghold; literally, a 'borough' or 'neighborhood'.

Carburized iron: A soft, impure form of steel.

Caulking: A fibrous mixture of animal hair and tar that is packed between two overlapping strakes in a ship, making the joint watertight.

Clinker-building: Building the shell of a boat with a series of overlapping strakes.

Coif: An item of head protection, usually a mail hood.

Crossbeam: A transverse timber spanning the hull of a vessel.

Danegeld: Tribute paid to Danish invaders in an attempt to stave off further attacks.

Danelaw: Regions of England to the north and east of Mercia that were occupied by the Danes in the 9th century.

Fyrd: The territorial levy of an Anglo-Saxon region.

Garboard: The first strake attached to the keel of a vessel.

Garniture: A set of armour with additional pieces that can be added or discarded according to necessity.

Godi: A priest. Jarls would assume this role at important religious ceremonies.

Gunnefane: War flag.

Halyard: A rope for raising and lowering the sail.

Heath-weru: Bodyguard.

Heeling: When a vessel leans over to one side due to pressure of the wind when under sail.

Hersir: A Scandinavian local leader. The word derives from *here*, a military host. Originally a freeholder but later becoming a form of royal official.

Hilt: The 'handle' of a sword consisting of the cross-guard, grip and pommel.

Hird: The territorial levy of a Scandinavian region.

Hogging: When pressure of the sea causes the bow and stern to droop and the vessel is in danger of breaking its back amidships.

Jarl: A Scandinavian regional ruler, usually the immediate subordinate of a king but sometimes independent.

Keelson: A longitudinal timber resting over the keel of a vessel.

Knarr: A substantial sea-going cargo vessel.

Lamellar: A type of armour made of small metal strips laced together.

Lands: The area where two strakes overlap in a vessel.

Ledungen: The local Scandinavian levy which the *jarl* was responsible for leading into battle.

Lenderman: A landed man; a noble.

Mail: Armour made from large numbers of small, interlinked iron rings.

Mast step: A fitting to locate the heel of the mast in the keelson.

Pattern-welding: A method of weapon manufacture by twisting rods of iron and carburized iron.

Pommel: The weighted end of a sword hilt, used to help counterbalance the blade.

Priare: A triple sheet attached to the middle lower edge of the sail.

Rabbet or rebate: A groove or step cut into a timber to receive the edge of another timber.

Ragnarok: In Norse mythology, the ultimate destruction of the gods in a cataclysmic battle with evil, out of which a new order will arise.

Rakke: A collar of rope or wood which keeps the yard attached to a ship's mast but allows vertical movement.

Reef: Reducing the area of the sail.

Reeve: An Anglo-Saxon minor royal official.

Rove: A small perforated metal plate through which a nail is passed then clenched over it.

Rowlock: A fulcrum for an oar fixed to the top of the gunwale.

Sax: A single-edged knife of anything up to sword length. Usually with a back thicker than the edge; the back often has an angled profile.

Scarf: An angled joint between two timbers.

Sheerstrake: The uppermost strake in the hull of a vessel.

Sheet: A rope fastened to lower corners of sail.

Shroud: A rope that supports the mast and runs from the masthead to the hull amidships.

Skald: A travelling poet.

Skjalborg (shield wall): A tightly arrayed body of warriors who are close enough to overlap shields in a mutually defensive barrier.

Skraelings: The collective term coined by the Vikings to describe indigenous people, particulary those of Vinland.

Stays: Ropes running from the masthead to the bow and stern to give longitudinal support to the mast.

Strake: A plank forming part of the side of a vessel.

Strandhögg: A coastal raid for supplies and profit.

Stringer: A wooden member running inboard fore and aft that gives longitudinal strength to a vessel's hull.

Svinfylka (swine array): An offensive formation of warriors fighting in a wedge shape.

Tacking: A manoeuvre by which a ship beats to windward.

Thing: A regional public assembly of land-owning freemen.

Thrall: A slave. Thralls were at the bottom of the Viking's social pyramid.

Thwart: A transverse bench or crossbeam.

Trenail: A round wooden peg sometimes slotted to take a wedge and used to fasten strakes to ribs and knees.

Vápnatak: The term for the mass display of weapon shaking that signalled the Icelanders' approval of the Althing's decision.

Varangian Guard: The personal bodyguard of the Byzantine emperor that initially consisted entirely of Scandinavian warriors.

Vinland: The name given by the Vikings to America.

Yard: A timber or spar from which the sail is suspended.

BIBLIOGRAPHY

Many of the most useful books on the subject are long out of print, but given that the majority of relevant information was known at the turn of the century, some of these more venerable works are still of value. The original 11th-century manuscripts containing the sagas are preserved at the Stofnun Arna Magnussonar, Reykjavik, Iceland.

Almgren, Bertil (ed), *The Viking* (Vitoria, 1975)

Arbman, Holger, *The Vikings* (1961)

Atkinson, Ian, *The Viking Ships* (1980)

Blake, N. F. (trans), *The Saga of the Jomsvikings* (Thomas Nelson and Sons, 1962)

Brogger, A. W. & Shetelig, H., *The Viking Ships* (Dreyers Forlag, Norway, 1951)

Brondsted, J., *The Vikings* (Penguin, 1960)

Donovan, Frank R., *The Vikings* (1970)

du Chaillu, P. B. (trans), *The Viking Age* (1889)

Farrell, R. T. (ed), *The Vikings* (1982)

Fitzhugh, W. & Ward, E. I. (eds), *Vikings: The North Atlantic Saga* (Smithsonian Press, 2000)

Foote, P. G. & Wilson, D. M., *The Viking Achievement* (Sidgwick and Jackson, 1970)

Garmonsway, G. N. (trans), *The Anglo-Saxon Chronicle* (1975)

Gibson, Michael, *The Vikings* (1972)

Graham-Campbell, James (ed), *Cultural Atlas of the Viking World* (Andromeda, 1994)

Graham-Campbell, James, *The Viking World* (Frances Lincoln, 1980)

Ingstad, Helge, *Westward to Vinland: The Discovery of Pre-Columbian Norse House Sites in North America* (Toronto, 1969)

Jensen, Ole Klindt & Ehren, Svenelov, *The World of the Vikings* (Allen and Unwin, 1970)

Jones, Gwyn, *A History of the Vikings* (Oxford University Press, 1968)

Kendrick, T. D., *A History of the Vikings* (1968)

Laing, Samuel (trans), *The Heimskringla* (J. M. Dent and Sons, 1930, in three volumes)

Lee, Thomas E., 'On the Trail of the Northmen', *The Beaver* (Winter, 1983)

Loyn, H. R., *The Vikings in Britain* (1977)

Magnusson, Magnus, *Viking Expansion Westwards* (1979)

Magnusson, Magnus & Pálsson, Hermann (trans), *Njal's Saga* (1971)

Magnusson, Magnus & Pálsson, Hermann (trans), *The Vinland Sagas: The Norse Discovery of America* (1965)

McGee, Robert, *Canada Rediscovered, Montreal and Ottawa* (1991)

Nørlund, Paul, *Viking Settlers in Greenland and Their Descendants during Five Hundred Years* (London and Copenhagen, 1936)

Oleson, T. J., *The Norsemen in North America* (Ottawa, 1963)

Oxenstierna, Eric, *The Norsemen* (1966)

Petersen, Jan, *De Norske Vikingesverd: En typologiskkronologisk studie over vikigetidens vaaben* (Kristiana, 1919)

Sawyer, P. H., *The Age of the Vikings* (1971)

Schlederman, Peter, 'Eskimo and Viking Finds in the High Arctic', *National Geographic* (May 1981)

Shetelig, Haakon (ed), *Viking Antiquities in Great Britain and Ireland* (Oslo, 1940, in six volumes)

Simpson, Jacqueline, *Everyday Life in the Viking Age* (1967)

Sjovold, Thorleif, *The Viking Ships in Oslo* (Universitetets Oldsaksamling, 1979)

Todd, J. H. (trans), *The War of the Gaedhil with the Gaill* (1867)

The Viking Ship Museum, *Sailing into the Past*, (Roskilde, Denmark, 1986)

Wilson, D. M., *The Vikings and Their Origins* (Thames and Hudson, 1970)

Wood, Michael, *In Search of the Dark Ages* (1981)

APPENDIX

MUSEUMS

Museums in England

British Museum

By far the best collection of Viking Age items in Britain. A tremendous variety of weapons but no helmets or mail shirts from this period. The collection of small finds is excellent, ranging from stirrups to pins. The Vikings Exhibition of 1980 saw the production of a useful catalogue: James Graham-Campbell and Dafydd Kidd, *The Vikings*, British Museum Publications, 1980. This details much Scandinavian and Continental material rarely seen in this country.

Museum of London

Good collection of weapons and an extensive collection of other Viking finds. An early but valuable catalogue of some of the best-known items was written by R. E. M. Wheeler: *London and the Vikings*, Museum of London, 1927.

Jorvik Centre/Archaeological Resource Centre, York

These are two separate museums, the first dedicated to the Viking settlement of Jorvik and the second an unusual glimpse into the various excavations in York. The Jorvik Centre includes a 'dark-ride' through a reconstructed section of the Coppergate area as it would have appeared in the middle of the 10th century. This gives a vivid impression of everyday Viking life. The small museum attached to the centre has some of the best-preserved textiles, shoes and small items in England. It should be borne in mind that civilian dress of this type would form the basic dress of the Viking warrior.

Scandinavian Museums

Statens Historiska Museum (Museum of National Antiquities), Stockholm

Contains not only the major Swedish finds of the Viking Age, but also items from the earlier Vendel/Valsgarde culture. As with many Scandinavian museums, a fine collection of English silver coinage is also held.

Universitetets Oldsaksamling (Museum of Cultural History), Oslo

The major Viking collection in Norway. Includes the Gjermundbu helmet.

Viking Ship Museum, Oslo

Holds the three impressive Viking ships from Oseberg, Gokstad and Tune, together with associated finds.

Nationalmuseet (National Museum of Denmark), Copenhagen
The largest collection of Danish material; not as impressive as the Swedish and Norwegian collections, but still of tremendous importance.

Vikingeskibshallen (Viking Ship Museum), Roskilde
Less than an hour from Copenhagen. Contains Viking vessels found in the Roskilde Fjord. Several reconstructed ships and audio-visual displays.

INDEX

References to illustrations are shown in **bold**.

Abbo of Fleury 99
Adam of Bremen 13
Adils 116
Aella, king of Northumbria 42
Aesir 36–7
aett 84–6
agriculture *see* farms and farming
Al-Tartushi 25
Alberich 137
Alcuin 10, 92
Alfgeir, Earl 115
Alfred, king of Wessex
    and *burhs* 106–8
    shipbuilding 181
    and the Vikings 43–5, 92, 100, 105
Althing 27–9, **28**
America *see* North America
amulets **25**, **121**, **123**
anchors 161, 169, 178, **190**
Andersen, Capt. Magnus 179
Anglo-Saxon Chronicle
    on Brunanburh (937) 115
    on Hardrada's invasion (1066) 59, 63–4
    name used for Vikings 13
    on Viking incursions into England 10, 40, 43, 46–7, 99, 101–2, 181
Anna Comnena 56
Annals of Innisfallen 50
Annals of St Neot 102, 106
L'Anse aux Meadows 72–3, **72**, **74**, **80**, 137
    artefacts **69**, **75**
Anwend 43
appearance 125–33
    see also clothing
archery 91–2, 95
    bows and arrows **90**
arm-rings **24**, **67**, **123**
armies
    levies 19, 180
    raising 105–6, 109
    standing 17
    transporting 180–1
armour 130–2
    7th century 125
    lamellar 130
    mail **58**, **62**, 75, **87**, **90**, **96**, 130, 138–8
    manufacture 138–9, **139**
Arnulf, king of Eastern Francia 45
Asgard 36, 38
Ashdown, battle of (871) 43, 94
Assembly *see* Thing
Athelney 43
Athelstan, king of Wessex 45, 100, 115, 116
axes **44**, **49**, **60**, **117**, 135–6, **135**

Baffin Island 78–80
Baldr 37, 38

Basil II, Byzantine emperor 56
battle tactics
    land 94–101
    sea 92–3, 188
Bayeux Tapestry scenes
    banquet preparations **31**
    colours 128
    Harold Godwinsson **19**
    Hastings **95**
    longships **180**
    shipbuilding **156**, **157**
    transporting horses in ships **101**
beads **16**
beds **28**, **144**
beiti-ass blocks **175**, 177, **190**, 191
Beorhtric, King 10, 82
berserkers 85, 102, **103**, 112
Birka 130
    finds **145**
Bjarni Herjolfsson 68, 192
blacksmiths 136–7, 157, 161
    forges **139**
'blood-eagle' death 42
boat ells 160
bodyguards *see* Huscarls; *Tinglith*; Varangian Guard
bóndis 19–22, **21**
Bothvar Bjarki 102
bowls **33**
bows and arrows **90**
    see also archery
bread 31–2
Brendan, Saint 65
Brennu-Njals Saga 133
Brian Boru, high king of Ireland 48–54
bridles **99**
Brodir of Man 50, 52
brooches **37**, **128**
Brunanburh (Vinheath), battle of (937) 100, 112–16, **114**
Burghal Hideage 106–8
burhs 106–8
burials
    ship *see* Gokstad ship; Ladby ship; Oseberg ship
    Valsgarde and Vendel 125, 129
Byhrtnoth, Ealdorman 116–20
Byzantine Empire 54–7, 59

camps 93, 99–100
cavalry 97–9
Charlemagne 12
children and childhood 20–1, 85–6
Chippenham 105
Christianity 40, 80, 121–2
Cimbri 10
Cinnamus 57
clans 84–6
cloak-pins **67**
cloaks 128
Clontarf, battle of (1014) 48–54, 103–4
clothing 125–8
    6th–7th centuries **14**
    8th–9th centuries **96**, **123**

9th–10th centuries **51**, **90**
10th–11th centuries **58**
12th century **62**, **83**, **97**
accessories 128
colours 128
Eastern Vikings **55**
making 24–5
women **26**
Cnut, king of England, Denmark and Norway **61**
bodyguard 91
clothing 126
and Danegeld 53
lineage 59
and ships 187
standards 101
coinage 18, **104**, **145**
combs 75, **126**
Conaing 52, 54
Constantinople 55, 56, 59
cooking 31–2, **31**
utensils **32**, 74
Corbridge, battle of (871) 94
Courland, harrying of 101, 105
Crumlin-Pedersen, Ole 154
Cuerdale hoard **104**

Danegeld 109
Danelaw 43–5
Danevirke 12
death
ship burials *see* Gokstad ship; Ladby ship; Oseberg ship
Valhalla 36, 38, **38**, **41**, 121
Valsgarde and Vendel burials 125, 129
deception 105
decking 167, 177, **190**, 191, 193
Denmark
domination of Norway 13
early overpopulation 15
farming 33
monarchy's emergence 12, 84
divorce 25
draughts, ships' 183, 186, 189
drekar 181
Droplaugarsona Saga 140–1
Dubhgall 50, 53
Dublin, kingdom of 42–3, 48–54
Dudo of St Quentin 123
dyes 128

Eadred, king of England 46
ealdormen 106
East Anglia, kingdom of 40, 42, 43, 45
Edington (Ethandun), battle of (878) 43
Edmund, St, king of East Anglia 42
Edward the Elder, king of Wessex 45
Edwin, earl of Mercia 60
Egil Skallagrimson 86, 101, 113–16, 124, 135–6
Egil's Saga 86, 100, 105, 111–12, 115–16
Einar Tambarskelf 91–2, 100
Elder Edda 84–5
Ellesmere Island 78

England
8th century 10, 82
9th–10th centuries 40–8, 99, 100, 106, 112–20
11th century 53, 58–65, 99
Anglo-Saxons in Varangian Guard 56–7
equipment 125–33
6th–7th centuries **14**
8th–9th centuries **96**, **123**
9th–10th centuries **51**, **90**
10th–11th centuries **58**
12th century **62**, **83**, **97**
Eric Bloodaxe 45–8, 124
Eric Hakonsson, Earl 94
Erik the Red 68, 192
see also Saga of Erik the Red
Erik the Victorious 90
Ethandun *see* Edington
Ethelred the Unready, king of England 58–9, 60, 120
Evenhus rock art 145
exploration voyages **12**, 65–81, **66**
conditions 192–3
re-enactments 179
Eyrbyggja Saga 140
Eystein Orri 63, 64
Ezra, Daniel 133

families, extended 84–6
farms and farming 20, 33–5, **34**
Fenrir 36, 38
feuds 20, 26, 125
figure heads
8th–9th centuries **152**, **153**
11th century **155**, **180**, **182**, **184**
Gokstad ship **174**
Oseberg ship 170–1
vanes **42**, **159**
Finnbogi 26
'Five Boroughs' 43, 45
Flateyjarbok **64**, 96
food and drink 31–3, 188
footwear 125–6
forging 136–7, **138**, **139**
formations, battle 92–101
fortifications 93, 99–100, 106–9, **107**, **108**
fostering 85–6
The Frankish Royal Annals 12–13
Franks Casket **13**
freemen *see bóndis*
Frey 37, 38
Freydis 26, 76
Freyja 37
Fulda Annals 101
Fulford, battle of (1066) 60–3
furniture **28**

Gaia **176**
games *see* sports and games
Ganga Hrolf 122–3
gangplanks 169, **175**, 178
Geats 10–12, 125
Geirmund Swathyskin 112

Georgios Maniakes 59
Giants of Frost and Fire 36, 38
gift economy 112–13, 121
Gisli Surson 141
Gisli's Saga 85
Gjermundbu helmet 129, **129**
glaives 135–6
Glenn Máma, battle of 49
Godfred of Denmark 12, 13
godi 19
gods and goddesses 36–40, 120–2
Gokstad ship 171–9, **175**
    artefacts **144**
    boats interred with 178–9, **178**
    burial chamber 171
    cross section **159**
    mast support system **159**
    reconstructions **143, 173, 175**
    replicas 154, **176**
    shields **132, 133, 174,** 176
Gotland picture stones 38, 41, 96, 132, 152, 168
government *see* kings; Thing
Great Dragon 181
Greenland
    Brattahild **67**
    exploration from 68–71, 75, 78, 133
    settlement of 67–8, 81, 192
    voyage from Norway 193
    winds and currents round 68
Gregory of Tours 12
Grettir Asmundson 86, 100
Grettir's Saga 92, 112
Groenlendinga ("Greenlanders") *Saga*
    on Freydis 26, 77
    on Viking exploration 67, 68, 71, 74–6
grooming 125
    combs **75, 126**
Gulathing Law 181
Gustafson, Prof. Gabriel 163
Guthfrith 45
Guthrum 43

Hafrsfjord, battle of (*c.* 872) 110–12, **111**, 182
Hakon, Earl 90
Hakon Sigurdsson, Earl 100
Half's Saga ok Halfsrekka 89
Halfdan Lodbrokson 40–3, 106
Halfdan the Black 110
halyards 163, **190**
Harald Bluetooth, king of Denmark 88
Harald Fairhair's Saga 102
Harald Hardrada *see* Harald Sigurdsson
Harald Harefoot, king of England 59
Harald Harfagri 110–12, 122
Harald Sigurdsson (Hardrada), king of Norway
    invasion of England (1066) 59–65, 95
    mail 130
    shipbuilding 181
    standard 105
    and Varangian Guard 56, 57, 59
Harold Godwinsson, king of England **19**, 59, 63–4

Harthacnut, king of England 59
Hastings, battle of (1066) 95
Hávamál ('Sayings of the High One') 40, 124
Havhingsten fra Glendalough **158, 186, 187**
'hazelled fields' 100
headgear 128
    see also helmets
Hedeby 25, 33
Heimdal 38
Heimskringla 98, 130, 132
Helge Ask **182, 183, 184**
Helgi 26
Helluland 68, 72
helmets 129–30
    7th century **14, 131**
    8th–9th centuries **96, 123**
    9th–10th centuries **44, 51, 90, 129**
    10th–11th centuries **58, 113**
    12th century **62, 83, 97**
    kettle **103**
Herring Strut-Haraldson 91
Hfransmal 102
bird 17, 89
Hirdskra 89, 105
Hjdrungavag, battle of (*c.* 990) 90
Hjortspring boat 146–8, **147**
hnefatafl 21, **22**
holds, ships' 191, 193
honour, sense of 20, 40
horse furniture **99**
horses 99, **101, 185**
houses 29–31, **34, 72, 74, 80**
Hring 115
Hrolf Kraki 102
Hubba Lodbrokson *see* Ubbi Lodbrokson
Huginn 36
hunting **19**, 92
Huscarls 63, 91, 130, 133, 135
Hygelac the Geat 10–12, 125

Ibn Fadlan 23, 25
Ibn Khordadbah 56
Iceland
    and berserkers 102
    government 27–9
    length of voyage from Norway 192
    and Saint Brendan 65
    settlement of 67
    Stöng farm complex **34**
    Thingvellir **28**
Imme Gram 183, 185
Indians, North American *see* Skraelings
Ingstad, Helge 72–3, 137
Inuits
    artefacts 78–80, **79**
    and Greenland 80, 81
    see also Skraelings
Ipswich 118
Ireland 42–3, 48–54, 99, 103–4
Ivar the Boneless 40–3

jarls 18–19

javelins 136
jewellery
    arm-rings **24**, **67**, **123**
    beads **16**
    brooches **37**, **128**
    cloak-pins **67**
    significance in gift economy 112
John of Wallingford 48
Jomsborg fortress 88–9, 90–1, **98**
Jomsvikings 87–91, **98**, 109, 118, 120
Jomsvikings' Saga 88–9
Jonsbok 181
Jordanes 10
Jotunheim 36

Karlsefni, Thorfinn *see* Thorfinn Karlsefni
karvi 142, 163–79
keels
    emergence of 149–50
    Gokstad ship 172
    knarrs 189, **190**, 193
    Oseberg ship 165
    preparing and laying 158
    Roskilde 6 187
keelsons
    9th century **159**
    definition 153
    Gokstad ship 173–4
    knarrs **190**, 191, 193
    making 155–6
    Oseberg ship 167–8
    Roskilde 6 187
    Skuldelev ships 185–6
Kerthjalfad 103–4
Kiev 55, 56
King Harald's Saga 59, 60–3, 64–5, 95
King Olaf Tryggvasson's Saga 64, 89–90, 94
kings
    emergence of Scandinavian monarchies 12, 13, 84
    growth in power 29
    origins of monarchy 122
    power and entourage 17–18
    selection 20, 27
kitchen utensils **32**, **74**
Kjotvi the Wealthy 112
knarrs 188–94, **194**
    cross section **192**
    definition 142
    plan **190**
    replicas **161**, **162**, 189, 192, **192**, 194, **195**
knives 134
Kormak's Saga 140
Kvalsund ship 149–50, **151**

Ladby ship 183
    replicas 183, **185**
Lambey Island 48
Landnámabok 193
law 27–9, 181
Laxdaela Saga 140
Leabhar Oiris 53

leadership, nature of 122–4
ledungen (levy) 19, 180
    ships 180–1, 184
Leif Eriksson 68–9
Leifsbudir 69, 70–1, 74
leisure *see* recreation
levy *see* ledungen
Lewis chessmen 97, **103**
'Life of St Aubin' **11**
Lindisfarne
    raid on (793) 10, 92
    tombstones **108**
livestock 35
logistics 105–9
Loki 37, 38
London Bridge, St Olaf's attack on (1014) 60
Long Serpent **94**, 109, 181
longhouses 29–31
long-saxes 134
longships **41**, 142–95
    11th century 179–87
    categorization 142, 181
    colours **183**
    early 144–51
    evolution 142
    levy ships 180–1, 184
    life on board 188, **190**
    Viking Age 152–79
    warships 180–8
lords
    role 112–13, 122
    see also kings
lycanthropy 102

Máelmórdha, king of Leinster 48–53
Magnus Barelegs 54
Magnus the Good, king of Denmark and Norway 59, 90–1
Maldon, battle of (991) 116–20
Mammen axe 135, **135**
Man, Isle of 50
Markland 69, 72
marriage 25
mast-fishes 153, **159**, 168, 174–5, **175**
masts
    knarrs **190**
    Oseberg ship 167–8
    supporting 152, **159**, 163, 167–8, 173–5, 180, **180**
meginhúfr 152, **159**, 165–6, 173
memorial stones **53**
mercenaries 113–16
Mercia, kingdom of 43
Meretun, battle of (871) 94
Michael Calaphates, Byzantine emperor 59
Midgard Serpent 36, **37**, 38, **53**
mints 18
monarchy *see* kings
monasteries: as targets for raids 82–4
money
    coinage 18, **104**, **145**
    Danegeld 109
    gift economy 112–13, 121

kings' finances 17–18
taxes 17
Montfaucon, battle of (888) 99
Mora 155
Morkere, earl of Northumbria 60
motivation 120–4
Munnin 36
Murchad 49–50, 51–4
mythology 36–40, 120–2, 136–7

Native Americans *see* Skraelings
naval battles and tactics 92–3, **94**, 188
navigation 192–3
Newfoundland *see* L'Anse aux Meadows
Nicolyasen, Nicolay 171
Njal's Saga 50, 51–2, 103–4, 125
Normandy 122–3
Norns 36
Norse Film and Pageant Society 96
North America 65–81, 133, 192
Northumbria, kingdom of 42, 43, 45, 106
see also York, kingdom of
Norway
early overpopulation 15
farming 33
monarchy's emergence 13
voyage to Greenland 193
voyage to Iceland 192
Novgorod 55
Nydam ship 148–9, **149**

oar holes
emergence of 153
Gokstad ship **159**, 175–6, **175**
knarrs 194
Oseberg ship 166
oars
emergence of 148–9
Gokstad ship **175**, 177
knarrs 192
numbers 161
Oseberg ship 169
oarsmen's seating 148, 150, 153, 169, 175, **182**, 184, **195**
Odin 36, 38, **38**, 120–1
advice to mankind 40, 124
and berserkers 102
and ravens 36, 104
Offa, king of Mercia 82
Olaf, king of Dublin 115
Olaf, king of York 45
Olaf Haraldsson (St Olaf), king of Norway **18**, 59, 60, 130, 132, 133
Olaf Sihtricsson, king of York 45
Olaf Tryggvasson, king of Norway
and Christianity 121
at Maldon (991) 118
ships **94**, 109, 181
standards 101
at Svöldr (1000) 90, **94**, 100, 141
weapons skills 91
see also *King Olaf Tryggvasson's Saga*
Olmütz helmet 130

Orkneyinga Saga 15–16, 103
Orkneys 45, 50, 65
Orosius 120
Oseberg ship 163–71, **166**
burial chamber 23, 164, **166**
constructing **159**
cross section **159**
finds **21**, **28**, **32**, **167**
restoration **164**, **170**
Oseberg tapestry 133
Oskytel 43
Ospak 50
Ostrogoths 10
Oswulf, earl of Bamburgh 47
Ottar **189**, **192**

parliament *see* Thing
pattern-welding 137
picture stones **38**, **41**, 96, 132, **152**, **168**
piecing 160, 165
Piraeus Lion **57**
place names 37, 45
planks, forming 156
plaques, whalebone **127**
ploughing 35
poets *see* skalds
prows 170–1, **182**
see also figure heads
psychology 20, 40, 120–4

Rafn, Prof. Carl Christian 67
Ragnar Lodbrok ('Hairy-breeches') 40–2, 106
Ragnar's Saga 40–2
Ragnarok 37, 38–40, 121
Ragnfrid, King 100
raids **90**
first 163
tactics and abilities 92, 93, 99
targets 82–4
Rathlin Island 48
Reachrainn 48
recreation 20–2
recruitment 109
reefing lines 162
religion 19, 35–40, 120–2
revenge *see* feuds
rewards system 112–13
rigging 162–3, 168–9, 177, **190**, 194
Roar Ege **161**, **162**, **194**
Rochester, siege of (885) 99, 100
Rognvald, king of York 45
Rollo (Rolf), duke of Normandy 123
ropes 163, **182**
Roskilde 179
see also Skuldelev ships
Roskilde 6 187
rowing benches 148, 150, 153, 169, 175, **182**, 184, **195**
rowlocks **149**
rudders
Gokstad ship 177–8
knarrs **190**

making 155
mounting fixed 150
Nydam ship **149**
Oseberg ship 169, **170**
Rus 54–7, **54**, **55**
etymology 13
Ibn Fadlan on 23, 25
shipbuilding **154**
weapons manufacture 137
Russia 54–6, 59, 117

Sabo, Deborah 78–80
sacrifices 35–6, 120
Saga of Erik the Red 67, 71, 75–7
sailing routes **12**
sailing speeds 185, 186, 194
sails 151
diamond-pattern **152**, 162, **168**
knarrs **190**, 191, 194
making 25, 161–3
Roskilde 6 188
Skuldelev ships 184, 186
Saint Olaf's Saga 60
St Wenceslas helmet 130
Saucourt, battle of (881) 97–8
scabbards 134
Scandinavia
state formations 12
see also Denmark; Norway; Sweden
scarfing 158, 165
Schledermann, Peter 78
Schonback, Bengt 73
sea battles and tactics 92–3, **94**, 188
Segurdur Stefansson 72
Sheppey, Isle of 40
shield racks, ships' 166–7, **175**
shield walls 94–6, **98**, **114**
shields 132–3
7th century **14**
8th–9th centuries **123**
9th–10th centuries **44**, **51**
10th–11th centuries **58**, **95**, **180**
12th century **62**, **83**, **97**
Gokstad **132**, **133**, **174**, 176
Vinlander colonists 74–5, 133
ship burials *see* Gokstad ship; Ladby ship; Oseberg ship
ships *see* longships
ships' boats 178–9, **178**, **180**, 192
shipwrights and shipbuilding
11th century 179–80, **182**
implements 156, 157, **157**, **159**, 160
Viking Age 154–63, **154**, **156–9**, **161**
shroud-pins **182**, **190**
signals *see* standards and signals
Sigtrygg Silkybeard, king of Dublin 48–50, 54
Sigtuna elk-antler carving 125, 129–30
Sigurd the Stout, earl of Orkney 50, 53, 103–4
Sigvaldi Strut-Haraldson, Earl 89, 90, 91
Sihtric, king of York 45
skalds 17–18
Skarphedin Njalson 91, 125, 126

Skraelings **70**, 71, 75–8, **78**, 81
Skuldelev ships 179, 185–8, 189–92, 193–4
Skuldelev 1 189–92, **191**
cross section **182**
replicas **189**, 192, **192**
Skuldelev 2 185–7
replicas **158**, 186–7, **186**, **187**
Skuldelev 3 193–4, **194**
replicas **161**, **162**, 194, **195**
Skuldelev 5 184–5
cross section **182**
replicas **182**, **183**, 184–5, **184**
slavery *see* thralls
Sleipnir 36, **38**
Snorri Sturlusson
on Norse religion 120–2
see also *Heimskringla*; *King Harald's Saga*
soapstone 33
society 15–27
extended family groupings 84–6
spears **88**, 136, **141**
9th–10th centuries **44**, **118**
9th–11th centuries **49**
decorated sockets **85**, **91**
sports and games 20–2, 86
Stamford Bridge, battle of (1066) 63–5, 95, 130
standards and signals 101–5
Steene, Anne 72–3
Stiklestad, battle of (1030) 59
strakes
4th century **148**
11th century **182**, 185
construction 158–60, **159**
Gokstad ship 172–3, 175, 176
knarrs 189, **190**
Oseberg ship 165–6
Roskilde 6 187
see also *meginhúfr*
strändhoggs **70**, 71
Strangford Lough, battle of (877) 43
Strathclyde British 115, 116
Strut-Harald, king of Scania 89
Styrbjorn Starki 90
Sulcoit, battle of (968) 99
Sulki, king of Rogaland 111–12
surprise attacks 105
Surt 38
Svein Asleifsson 15–16
Svein Ulfsson 59
Sverri's Saga 57, 105
Svöldr, battle of (1000) 90, **94**, 100, 102, 109, 141, 182
Sweden
and the East 54–6
farming 33
Swein Forkbeard, king of England and Denmark 59, 88–9, 90, 107
'swine arrays' 96–7, **114**
swords 46, **47**, **84**, 86, **88**, **123**, 134
8th–9th centuries **123**
9th–10th centuries **44**
longevity 141
makers' marks **134**

manufacture and repair 136–7, 139–41
   pommel caps **141**

tactics 92–105, 188
Tadg 52
taxes 17
Teutones 10
Thanet, Isle of 40
Thidrik's Saga 136–7
Thing 19, 27–9, **27**
Thor 36–7, 38, **39**
Thord Granison 86
Thorfinn Karlsefni 74–6
Thorir Longchin 112
Thorkell the Tall 53, 91, 109, 118
Thorolf Kvendulfson 112
Thorolf Skallagrimson 101, 115–16
Thorvald Eriksson 70–1
Thorvard 26
thralls 22–3, 31
   capturing **70**
Tilia 147
timber
   felling 156, **157**
   forming planks from 156
   shipbuilding types 154–6, 180
   shipbuilding uses 156–7
Tinglith 91
Toirdelbach 52, 54
Tosti 53
Tostig, earl of Northumbria 59–65
trading routes **12**
trading ships *see knarrs*
training 84–92, **98**
transport
   armies 180–1
   land 109
travel
   at home 35
   see also voyages
Trelleborg fortresses **107**, 108–9, **110**
tribes 84–6
trickery 105
trousers **51**, 126–7
tunics **51**, 127–8
Turgesius (Turgeis) 48
Tyr 120

Ubbi (Hubba) Lodbrokson 40–2, 104, 106
Ulf 53
umiaks 145
Uppland **53**

Valhalla 36, 38, **38**, **41**, 121
Valkyries 36, **38**
Valsgarde burial 125, 129
Vanir 37
vápnatak 29
Varangian Guard 54–7, **54**, **55**, 59
Vendel burial 125, 129
Vestfold 110–11

Vidar 38
Viking 154, 179
Vikings
   Anglo-Saxon names for 13
   etymology 13–15
   origins 15
Villehardouin 57
Vinheath *see* Brunanburh
Vinland 69–78, 133
Vinland map 72
violence, attitude to 86, 120–1
Visigoths 10
Vitlycke rock art **146**
Vladimir of Kiev 56
Volsunga Saga 102
Volund the Smith 136–7
voyages
   conditions 188, **190**, 192–3
   of exploration **12**, 65–81, **66**
   re-enactments 179
   sailing speeds 185, 186, 194
   ships 142–95

Wallace, Brigitta 73
War of the Gaedhil with the Gaill 52
warriors
   6th–7th centuries **14**
   8th–9th centuries **96**, **123**
   9th–10th centuries **51**, **90**
   10th–11th centuries **58**
   12th century **62**, **83**, **97**
   Eastern **55**
   Skraelings as 76–7
   and Valhalla 36, 38, **38**, **41**, 121
water supply, ships' 178
weapons 133–41
   axes **44**, **49**, **60**, **117**, 135–6, **135**
   bows and arrows **90**
   glaives 135–6
   javelins 136
   knives 134
   long-saxes 134
   manufacture and repair 136–41, **138**, **139**
   Skraelings 76–7
   Vinlander colonists 74
   see also spears; swords
Wessex, kingdom of 43–5, 106–8
Western Isles 45, 50, 65
William I the Conqueror, king of England: flagship **155**
Winchester New Minster **61**
wolfcoats *see* berserkers
women 24–7, **25**, **26**
   thralls 23
wood *see* timber

Yggdrasill 36, 38
Ymma Aelgyfu, queen of England **61**
Ynglinga Saga 102
York
   and Hardrada 63
   kingdom of 42, 45–8, 106